EVERYMAN,

I WILL GO WITH THEE

AND BE THY GUI   ,

HY

EVERYMAN'S LIBRARY
POCKET POETS

Animal Poems

Selected and edited by
John Hollander

E V E R Y M A N ' S   L I B R A R Y

P O C K E T   P O E T S

Alfred A. Knopf · New York · Toronto

THIS IS A BORZOI BOOK

PUBLISHED BY ALFRED A. KNOPF, INC.

This selection by John Hollander first published in
Everyman's Library, 1994
Copyright © 1994 by David Campbell Publishers Ltd.
Second printing

ISBN 0-679-43631-6

Typography by Peter B. Willberg

Typeset in the UK by MS Filmsetting Ltd., Frome, Somerset

Printed and bound in Italy by
Rotolito Lombarda S.p.A.

CONTENTS

THE HUNTED AND THEIR HUNTERS

SOME WINGED PREDATORS

CREATURES SMALL

ALL CREATURES

FOREWORD

Poets have written about animals since ancient times, and the poems I have chosen here cover two thousand years, from lines of Lucretius, Virgil and Oppian to those of the romantics like Wordsworth, Blake, Whitman and Dickinson; from moderns like D. H. Lawrence and Marianne Moore to contemporaries like James Merrill. In most languages, there are many more poems about insects and birds and sea-creatures than about mammals. And there are more about wild or strange animals than about familiar ones (save, perhaps, for the most familiar, the creatures of our households, the dogs and cats). Prior to colonial exploration and the rise of the study of natural science, which made creatures like panthers more familiar, the poet had more room for fancy. (The weird lore of medieval bestiaries could completely confound biological reality.) But there is a history of poetry as well as a history of biological knowledge. European Renaissance poems tended to treat animals symbolically and to moralize upon them. Romantic and modern poems acknowledge both a fascinating otherness and a deeper kinship with wild or strange creatures; most characteristic of more recent poetry has been the particular encounter between a human person and an animal presence, generating fables of a more complex sort than mere emblems.

13

But poetry antedates zoology and the taxonomy of these poems is only partially biological, and ranges from domestic companions to animals generally viewed across scientific distance. The aquatic creatures here addressed, for example, include mammals, fish, crustacea and others; but it is their common element which groups them poetically. On the other hand, it seemed right to allow the bat to associate with other small mammals its body resembles, as the crow with birds of prey.

I have placed these poems, from several eastern and western languages, in their categorical cages. But they are not locked up there, and the reader will want, in memory and interpretation, to move them meditatively about. Sometimes they will be associated by virtue of whether the animal speaks its piece in the first person, or is addressed, invoked, queried, scrutinized or allegorized; sometimes poems on the same animal will be adjacent; sometimes with intervening poems on related other creatures between them.

In the case of some poems, I have added titles, either when there were none originally (as in Emily Dickinson's poems) or when the selection is from a longer work (such as Virgil's Georgics).

JOHN HOLLANDER

HOUSEHOLDERS

CATS AND DOG

DOG The single creature leads a partial life,
      Man by his mind, and by his nose the hound;
      He needs the deep emotions I can give,
      I scent in him a vaster hunting ground.

CATS Like calls to like, to share is to relieve
      And sympathy the root bears love the flower;
      He feels in us, and we in him perceive
      A common passion for the lonely hour.

CATS We move in our apartness and our pride
      About the decent dwellings he has made:
DOG In all his walks I follow at his side,
      His faithful servant and his loving shade.

CAT

She sights a Bird – she chuckles –
She flattens – then she crawls –
She runs without the look of feet –
Her eyes increase to Balls –

Her Jaws stir – twitching – hungry –
Her Teeth can hardly stand –
She leaps, but Robin leaped the first –
Ah, Pussy, of the Sand,

The Hopes so juicy ripening –
You almost bathed your Tongue –
When Bliss disclosed a hundred Toes –
And fled with every one –

ENGLISH COCKER: OLD AND BLIND

With what painful deliberation he comes down the
    stair,
At the edge of each step one paw suspended in air,
And distrust. Does he thus stand on a final edge
Of the world? Sometimes he stands thus, and will not
    budge,

With a choking soft whimper, while monstrous
    blackness is whirled
Inside his head, and outside too, the world
Whirling in blind vertigo. But if your hand
Merely touches his head, old faith comes flooding back
    – and

The paw descends. His trust is infinite
In you, who are, in his eternal night,
Only a frail scent subject to the whim
Of wind, or only a hand held close to him

With a dog biscuit, or, in a sudden burst
Of temper, the force that jerks that goddamned,
    accurst
Little brute off your bed. But remember how you last
    saw
Him hesitate in his whirling dark, one paw

Suspended above the abyss at the edge of the stair,
And remember that musical whimper, and how, then
    aware
Of a sudden sweet heart-stab, you knew in him
The kinship of all flesh defined by a halting paradigm.

BLACK CAT

A ghost, though invisible, still is like a place
your sight can knock on, echoing; but here
within this thick black pelt, your strongest gaze
will be absorbed and utterly disappear:

just as a raving madman, when nothing else
can ease him, charges into his dark night
howling, pounds on the padded wall, and feels
the rage being taken in and pacified.

She seems to hide all looks that have ever fallen
into her, so that, like an audience,
she can look them over, menacing and sullen,
and curl to sleep with them. But all at once

as if awakened, she turns her face to yours;
and with a shock, you see yourself, tiny,
inside the golden amber of her eyeballs
suspended, like a prehistoric fly.

RAINER MARIA RILKE

TRANSLATED BY STEPHEN MITCHELL

THE MONGREL

In Havenpool Harbour the ebb was strong,
And a man with a dog drew near and hung,
And taxpaying day was coming along,
    So the mongrel had to be drowned.
The man threw a stick from the paved wharf-side
Into the midst of the ebbing tide,
And the dog jumped after with ardent pride
    To bring the stick aground.

But no: the steady suck of the flood
To seaward needed, to be withstood,
More than the strength of mongrelhood
    To fight its treacherous trend.
So, swimming for life with desperate will,
The struggler with all his natant skill
Kept buoyant in front of his master, still
    There standing to wait the end.

The loving eyes of the dog inclined
To the man he held as a god enshrined,
With no suspicion in his mind
    That this had all been meant.
Till the effort not to drift from shore
Of his little legs grew slower and slower,
And, the tide still outing with brookless power,
    Outward the dog, too, went.

Just ere his sinking what does one see
Break on the face of that devotee?
A wakening to the treachery
    He had loved with love so blind?
The faith that had shone in that mongrel's eye
That his owner would save him by and by
Turned to much like a curse as he sank to die,
    And a loathing of mankind.

CATS

Lovers, scholars – the fervent, the austere –
grow equally fond of cats, their household pride.
As sensitive as either to the cold,
as sedentary, though so strong and sleek,

your cat, a friend to learning and to love,
seeks out both silence and the awesome dark . . .
Hell would have made the cat its courier
could it have controverted feline pride!

Dozing, all cats assume the svelte design
of desert sphinxes sprawled in solitude,
apparently transfixed by endless dreams;

their teeming loins are rich in magic sparks,
and golden specks like infinitesimal sand
glisten in those enigmatic eyes.

CHARLES BAUDELAIRE
        TRANSLATED BY RICHARD HOWARD

THE CAT AND THE MOON

The cat went here and there
And the moon spun round like a top,
And the nearest kin of the moon,
The creeping cat, looked up.
Black Minnaloushe stared at the moon,
For, wander and wail as he would,
The pure cold light in the sky
Troubled his animal blood.
Minnaloushe runs in the grass
Lifting his delicate feet.
Do you dance, Minnaloushe, do you dance?
When two close kindred meet,
What better than call a dance?
Maybe the moon may learn,
Tired of that courtly fashion,
A new dance turn.
Minnaloushe creeps through the grass
From moonlit place to place,
The sacred moon overhead
Has taken a new phase.
Does Minnaloushe know that his pupils
Will pass from change to change,
And that from round to crescent,
From crescent to round they range?

Minnaloushe creeps through the grass
Alone, important and wise,
And lifts to the changing moon
His changing eyes.

MY CAT JEOFFRY

For I will consider my Cat Jeoffry.

For he is the servant of the Living God duly and daily
    serving him.

For at the first glance of the glory of God in the East
    he worships in his way.

For is this done by wreathing his body seven times
    round with elegant quickness.

For then he leaps up to catch the musk, which is the
    blessing of God upon his prayer.

For he rolls upon the prank to work it in.

For having done duty and received blessing he begins
    to consider himself.

For this he performs in ten degrees.

For first he looks upon his fore-paws to see if they are
    clean.

For secondly he kicks up behind to clear away there.

For thirdly he works it upon stretch with the fore-
    paws extended.

For fourthly he sharpens his paws by wood.

For fifthly he washes himself.

For Sixthly he rolls upon wash.

For Seventhly he fleas himself, that he may not be
    interrupted upon the beat.

For Eighthly he rubs himself against a post.

For Ninthly he looks up for his instructions.

For Tenthly he goes in quest of food.

For having consider'd God and himself he will consider his neighbour.

For if he meets another cat he will kiss her in kindness.

For when he takes his prey he plays with it to give it a chance.

For one mouse in seven escapes by his dallying.

For when his day's work is done his business more properly begins.

For he keeps the Lord's watch in the night against the adversary.

For he counteracts the powers of darkness by his electrical skin & glaring eyes.

For he counteracts the Devil, who is death, by brisking about the life.

For in his morning orisons he loves the sun and the sun loves him.

For he is of the tribe of Tiger.

For the Cherub Cat is a term of the Angel Tiger.

For he has the subtlety and hissing of a serpent, which in goodness he suppresses.

For he will not do destruction if he is well-fed, neither will he spit without provocation.

For he purrs in thankfulness, when God tells him he's a good Cat.

For he is an instrument for the children to learn benevolence upon.

For every house is incompleat without him & a
   blessing is lacking in the spirit.

For the Lord commanded Moses concerning the cats at
   the departure of the Children of Israel from
   Egypt.

For every family had one cat at least in the bag.

For the English Cats are the best in Europe.

For he is the cleanest in the use of his fore-paws of any
   quadrupede.

For the dexterity of his defence is an instance of the
   love of God to him exceedingly.

For he is the quickest to his mark of any creature.

For he is tenacious of his point.

For he is a mixture of gravity and waggery.

For he knows that God is his Saviour.

For there is nothing sweeter than his peace when at
   rest.

For there is nothing brisker than his life when in
   motion.

For he is of the Lord's poor and so indeed is he called
   by benevolence perpetually – Poor Jeoffry! poor
   Jeoffry! the rat has bit thy throat.

For I bless the name of the Lord Jesus that Jeoffry is
   better.

For the divine spirit comes about his body to sustain it
   in compleat cat.

For his tongue is exceeding pure so that it has in purity
   what it wants in musick.

For he is docile and can learn certain things.

For he can set up with gravity which is patience upon approbation.

For he can fetch and carry, which is patience in employment.

For he can jump over a stick which is patience upon proof positive.

For he can spraggle upon waggle at the word of command.

For he can jump from an eminence into his master's bosom.

For he can catch the cork and toss it again.

For he is hated by the hyprocrite and miser.

For the former is afraid of detection.

For the latter refuses the charge.

For he camels his back to bear the first notion of business.

For he is good to think on, if a man would express himself neatly.

For he made a great figure in Egypt for his signal services.

For he killed the Icneumon-rat very pernicious by land.

For his ears are so acute that they sting again.

For from this proceeds the passing quickness of his attention.

For by stroking him I have found out electricity.

For I perceived God's light about him both wax and
    fire.
For the Electrical fire is the spiritual substance, which
    God sends from heaven to sustain the bodies both
    of man and beast.
For God has blessed him in the variety of his
    movements.
For, tho' he cannot fly, he is an excellent clamberer.
For his motions upon the face of the earth are more
    than any other quadrupede.
For he can tread to all the measures upon the musick.
For he can swim for life.
For he can creep.

ODE ON THE DEATH OF A FAVOURITE CAT, DROWNED IN A TUB OF GOLD FISHES

'Twas on a lofty vase's side,
Where China's gayest art had dyed
   The azure flowers, that blow;
Demurest of the tabby kind,
The pensive Selima reclined,
   Gazed on the lake below.

Her conscious tail her joy declared;
The fair round face, the snowy beard,
   The velvet of her paws,
Her coat that with the tortoise vies,
Her ears of jet and emerald eyes,
   She saw; and purred applause.

Still had she gazed; but 'midst the tide
Two angel forms were seen to glide,
   The Genii of the stream:
Their scaly armour's Tyrian hue
Through richest purple to the view
   Betrayed a golden gleam.

The hapless nymph with wonder saw:
A whisker first and then a claw,
　　With many an ardent wish,
She stretched in vain to reach the prize.
What female heart can gold despise?
　　What cat's averse to fish?

Presumptuous maid! with looks intent
Again she stretched, again she bent,
　　Nor knew the gulf between.
(Malignant Fate sat by and smiled)
The slippery verge her feet beguiled,
　　She tumbled headlong in.

Eight times emerging from the flood
She mewed to every watery god,
　　Some speedy aid to send.
No dolphin came, no Nereid stirred:
Nor cruel Tom nor Susan heard.
　　A favourite has no friend!

From hence, ye beauties, undeceived,
Know, one false step is ne'er retrieved,
　　And be with caution bold.
Not all that tempts your wandering eyes
And heedless hearts is lawful prize;
　　Nor all that glisters gold.

THOMAS GRAY　　　　　　　　　　　　　　　33

ON THE DEATH OF ECHO,
A FAVOURITE BEAGLE

Silent at last, beneath the silent ground,
Here Echo lives, no unsubstantial sound
Nor babbling mimic – but a Beagle fleet
With drooping ears, keen nose, and nimble feet.
In the glad Chase she raised her merry voice
And made her name-sake of the woods rejoice,
But now dumb Death has chok'd poor Echo's cry
And to no call can Echo more reply –

LAST WORDS TO A DUMB FRIEND

Pet was never mourned as you,
Purrer of the spotless hue,
Plumy tail, and wistful gaze
While you humoured our queer ways,
Or outshrilled your morning call
Up the stairs and through the hall –
Foot suspended in its fall –
While, expectant, you would stand
Arched, to meet the stroking hand;
Till your way you chose to wend
Yonder, to your tragic end.

Never another pet for me!
Let your place all vacant be;
Better blankness day by day
Than companion torn away.
Better bid his memory fade,
Better blot each mark he made,
Selfishly escape distress
By contrived forgetfulness,
Than preserve his prints to make
Every morn and eve an ache.

From the chair whereon he sat
Sweep his fur, nor wince thereat;
Rake his little pathways out
Mid the bushes roundabout;
Smooth away his talons' mark
From the claw-worn pine-tree bark,
Where he climbed as dusk embrowned,
Waiting us who loitered round.

Strange it is this speechless thing,
Subject to our mastering,
Subject for his life and food
To our gift, and time, and mood;
Timid pensioner of us Powers,
His existence ruled by ours,
Should – by crossing at a breath
Into safe and shielded death,
By the merely taking hence
Of his insignificance –
Loom as largened to the sense,
Shape as part, above man's will,
Of the Imperturbable.

As a prisoner, flight debarred,
Exercising in a yard,
Still retain I, troubled, shaken,
Mean estate, by him forsaken;
And this home, which scarcely took
Impress from his little look,
By his faring to the Dim
Grows all eloquent of him.

Housemate, I can think you still
Bounding to the window-sill,
Over which I vaguely see
Your small mound beneath the tree,
Showing in the autumn shade
That you moulder where you played.

THOSE WE
BREED

HORSES

Those lumbering horses in the steady plough,
On the bare field – I wonder why, just now,
They seemed terrible, so wild and strange,
Like magic power on the stony grange.

Perhaps some childish hour has come again,
When I watched fearful, through the blackening rain,
Their hooves like pistons in an ancient mill
Move up and down, yet seem as standing still.

Their conquering hooves which trod the stubble down
Were ritual that turned the field to brown,
And their great hulks were seraphim of gold,
Or mute ecstatic monsters on the mould.

And oh the rapture, when, one furrow done,
They marched broad-breasted to the sinking sun!
The light flowed off their bossy sides in flakes;
The furrows rolled behind like struggling snakes.

But when at dusk with steaming nostrils home
They came, they seemed gigantic in the gloom,
And warm and glowing with mysterious fire
That lit their smouldering bodies in the mire.

Their eyes as brilliant and as wide as night
Gleamed with a cruel apocalyptic light.
Their manes the leaping ire of the wind
Lifted with rage invisible and blind.

Ah, now it fades! it fades! and I must pine
Again for that dread country crystalline,
Where the blank field and the still-standing tree
Were bright and fearful presences to me.

THE COW IN APPLE TIME

Something inspires the only cow of late
To make no more of a wall than an open gate,
And think no more of wall-builders than fools.
Her face is flecked with pomace and she drools
A cider syrup. Having tasted fruit,
She scorns a pasture withering to the root.
She runs from tree to tree where lie and sweeten
The windfalls spiked with stubble and worm-eaten.
She leaves them bitten when she has to fly.
She bellows on a knoll against the sky.
Her udder shrivels and the milk goes dry.

THE CALF

You may have seen, in road or street
    At times, when passing by,
A creature with bewildered bleat
Behind a milcher's tail, whose feet
    Went pit-pat. That was I.

Whether we are of Devon kind,
    Shorthorns, or Herefords,
We are in general of one mind
That in the human race we find
    Our masters and our lords.

When grown up (if they let me live)
    And in a dairy-home,
I may less wonder and misgive
Than now, and get contemplative,
    And never wish to roam.

And in some fair stream, taking sips,
    May stand through summer noons,
With water dribbling from my lips
And rising halfway to my hips,
    And babbling pleasant tunes.

KNOWING ABOUT HORSES
from Georgics, Book III

    Like diligence requires the courser's race,
In early choice, and for a longer space.
The colt that for a stallion is design'd
By sure presages shows his generous kind;
Of able body, sound of limb and wind.
Upright he walks, on pasterns firm and straight;
His motions easy; prancing in his gait;
The first to lead the way, to tempt the flood,
To pass the bridge unknown, nor fear the trembling
      wood;
Dauntless at empty noises; lofty neck'd,
Sharp-headed, barrel-bellied, broadly back'd;
Brawny his chest, and deep; his colour grey;
For beauty, dappled, or the brightest bay:
Faint white and dun will scarce the rearing pay.
    The fiery courser, when he hears from far
The sprightly trumpets and the shouts of war,
Pricks up his ears; and, trembling with delight,
Shifts place, and paws, and hopes the promis'd fight.
On his right shoulder his thick mane, reclin'd,
Ruffles at speed, and dances in the wind.
His horny hoofs are jetty black and round;

His chine is double; starting, with a bound
He turns the turf, and shakes the solid ground.
Fire from his eyes, clouds from his nostrils flow:
He bears his rider headlong on the foe.

PIG

In the manger of course were cows and the Child
     Himself
          Was like unto a lamb
Who should come in the fulness of time on an ass's
     back
          Into Jerusalem

And all things be redeemed – the suckling babe
          Lie safe in the serpent's home
And the lion eat straw like the ox and roar its love
          to Mark and to Jerome

And God's Peaceable Kingdom return among them all
          Save one full of offense
Into which the thousand fiends of a human soul
          Were cast and driven hence

And the one thus cured gone up into the hills
          To worship and to pray:
O Swine that takest away our sins
          That takest away

ANTHONY HECHT

RIDING A NERVOUS HORSE

A dozen false starts:
You're such a fool, I said,
Spooking at shadows when
All day you were calm,
Placidly nosing the bushes
That now you pretend are strange,
Are struck with menace.

But he shuddered, stubborn
In his horsy posture,
Saying that I brought
Devils with me that he
Could hear gathering in all
The places behind him as I
Diverted his coherence
With my chatter and tack.

Indeed I have stolen
Something, a careful attention
I claim for my own yearning
Purpose, while he
Is left alone to guard
Us both from horse eaters
That merely grin at me
But lust for him, for

The beauty of the haunch
My brush has polished, revealing
Treasures of edible light
In the shift of hide and hooves.

THE OXEN

Christmas Eve, and twelve of the clock.
   'Now they are all on their knees,'
An elder said as we sat in a flock
   By the embers in hearthside ease.

We pictured the meek mild creatures where
   They dwelt in their strawy pen,
Nor did it occur to one of us there
   To doubt they were kneeling then.

So fair a fancy few would weave
   In these years! Yet, I feel,
If someone said on Christmas Eve,
   'Come; see the oxen kneel

'In the lonely barton by yonder coomb
   Our childhood used to know,'
I should go with him in the gloom,
   Hoping it might be so.

THE DONKEY

When fishes flew and forests walked
   And figs grew upon thorn,
Some moment when the moon was blood,
   Then surely I was born;

With monstrous head and sickening cry
   And ears like errant wings,
The devil's walking parody
   On all four-footed things.

The tattered outlaw of the earth,
   Of ancient crooked will;
Starve, scourge, deride me: I am dumb,
   I keep my secret still.

Fools! For I also had my hour;
   One far fierce hour and sweet:
There was a shout about my ears,
   And palms before my feet!

G. K. CHESTERTON

MURMURING OF
INNUMERABLE
BEES

BEES

Bees are Black, with Gilt Surcingles –
Buccaneers of Buzz.
Ride abroad in ostentation
And subsist on Fuzz.

Fuzz ordained – not Fuzz contingent –
Marrows of the Hill.
Jugs – a Universe's fracture
Could not jar or spill.

OF BEES
from Georgics, Book IV

Of all the race of animals, alone,
The bees have common cities of their own;
And, common sons, beneath one law they live,
And with one common stock their traffic drive.
Each has a certain home, a sev'ral stall;
All is the State's, the State provides for all.
Mindful of coming cold, they share the pain,
And hoard, for winter's use, the summer's gain.
Some o'er the public magazines preside,
And some are sent new forage to provide;
These drudge in fields abroad, and those at home
Lay deep foundations for the labor'd comb,
With dew, narcissus leaves, and clammy gum.
To pitch the waxen flooring some contrive;
Some nurse the future nation of the hive;
Sweet honey some condense; some purge the grout;
The rest, in cells apart, the liquid nectar shut:
All, with united force, combine to drive
The lazy drones from the laborious hive;
With envy stung, they view each other's deeds;
With diligence the fragrant work proceeds.
As when the Cyclops, at th' almighty nod,
New thunder hasten for their angry god,
Subdued in fire the stubborn metal lies;

One brawny smith the puffing bellows plies,
And draws and blows reciprocating air:
Others to quench the hissing mass prepare;
With lifted arms they order ev'ry blow,
And chime their sounding hammers in a row;
With labor'd anvils Ætna groans below:
Strongly they strike; huge flakes of flames expire;
With tongs they turn the steel, and vex it in the fire.
If little things with great we may compare,
Such are the bees, and such their busy care;
Studious of honey, each in his degree,
The youthful swain, the grave experienc'd bee:
That in the field; this, in affairs of state
Employ'd at home, abides within the gate,
To fortify the combs, to build the wall,
To prop the ruins, lest the fabric fall:
But, late at night, with weary pinions come
The lab'ring youth, and heavy laden, home.
Plains, meads, and orchards, all the day he plies;
The gleans of yellow thyme distend his thighs:
He spoils the saffron flow'rs; he sips the blues
Of vi'lets, wilding blooms, and willow dews.
Their toil is common, common is their sleep;
They shake their wings when morn begins to peep,
Rush thro' the city gates without delay,
Nor ends their work, but with declining day.
Then, having spent the last remains of light,

They give their bodies due repose at night,
When hollow murmurs of their ev'ning bells
Dismiss the sleepy swains, and toll 'em to their cells.
When once in beds their weary limbs they steep,
No buzzing sounds disturb their golden sleep.

TRANSLATED BY JOHN DRYDEN

THE HUMBLE-BEE

Burly, dozing, humble-bee,
Where thou art is clime for me.
Let them sail for Porto Rique,
Far-off heats through seas to seek;
I will follow thee alone,
Thou animated torrid-zone!
Zigzag steerer, desert cheerer,
Let me chase thy waving lines;
Keep me nearer, me thy hearer,
Singing over shrubs and vines.

Insect lover of the sun,
Joy of thy dominion!
Sailor of the atmosphere;
Swimmer through the waves of air;
Voyager of light and noon;
Epicurean of June;
Wait, I prithee, till I come
Within earshot of thy hum, –
All without is martyrdom.

When the south wind, in May days,
With a net of shining haze
Silvers the horizon wall,
And, with softness touching all,

Tints the human countenance
With a colour of romance,
And, infusing subtle heats,
Turns the sod to violets,
Thou, in sunny solitudes,
Rover of the underwoods,
The green silence dost displace
With thy mellow, breezy bass.

Hot midsummer's petted crone,
Sweet to me thy drowsy tone
Tells of countless sunny hours,
Long days, and solid banks of flowers;
Of gulfs of sweetness without bound
In Indian wildernesses found;
Of Syrian peace, immortal leisure,
Firmest cheer, and bird-like pleasure.

Aught unsavoury or unclean
Hath my insect never seen;
But violets and bilberry bells,
Maple-sap, and daffodels,
Grass with green flag half-mast high,
Succory to match the sky,
Columbine with horn of honey,
Scented fern, and agrimony,
Clover, catchfly, adder's tongue,

And brier roses, dwelt among;
All beside was unknown waste,
All was picture as he passed.

Wiser far than human seer,
Yellow-breeched philosopher!
Seeing only what is fair,
Sipping only what is sweet,
Thou dost mock at fate and care,
Leave the chaff, and take the wheat.
When the fierce north-western blast
Cools sea and land so far and fast,
Thou already slumberest deep;
Woe and want thou canst outsleep;
Want and woe, which torture us,
Thy sleep makes ridiculous.

THE BEE
To Francis de Miomandre

What and how keen and mortal soever
Your sting may be, blond bee,
Over my tender basket I've thrown
Only a mere dream of lace.

Prick the gourd of the lovely breast
Where love lies dead or asleep,
So that a little of my red
May rise in the round resistant flesh!

I greatly need an instant pang:
A vivid and a clear-cut pain
Is better than a drowsy torment.

So let my senses be illumined
By that tiniest golden alert
For lack of which Love dies or sleeps!

        TRANSLATED BY DAVID PAUL

IN THE OPEN
FIRMAMENT OF
HEAVEN

ROBIN

The robin is a Gabriel
In humble circumstances,
His dress denotes him socially
Of transport's working classes.
He has the punctuality
Of the New England farmer –
The same oblique integrity,
A vista vastly warmer.
A small but sturdy residence,
A self-denying household,
The guests of perspicacity
Are all that cross his threshold.
As covert as a fugitive,
Cajoling consternation
By ditties to the enemy,
And sylvan punctuation.

THE LARK'S SONG

Thou hearest the Nightingale begin the Song of
    Spring;
The lark sitting upon his earthy bed, just as the morn
Appears, listens silent, then springing from the waving
    Corn-field, loud
He leads the Choir of Day-trill, trill, trill, trill,
Mounting upon the wing of light into the Great
    Expanse,
Re-echoing against the lovely blue and shining
    heavenly Shell,
His little throat labours with inspiration, every feather
On throat and breast and wings vibrates with the
    effluence Divine.
All nature listens silent to him, and the awful Sun
Stands still upon the Mountain looking on this little
    Bird
With eyes of soft humility and wonder, love, and awe.

THE MOCKING BIRD
from 'A Journey from Patapsko to Annapolis'

But what is *He*, who perch'd above the rest,
Pours out such various Musick from his Breast!
His Breast, whose Plumes a cheerful White display,
His quiv'ring Wings are dress'd in sober Grey.
Sure, all the *Muses*, this their Bird inspire!
And *He*, alone, is equal to the Choir
Of warbling Songsters who around him play,
While, Echo like, *He* answers ev'ry Lay.
The chirping *Lark* now sings with sprightly Note,
Responsive to her Strain *He* shapes his Throat:
Now the poor widow'd *Turtle* wails her Mate,
While in soft Sounds *He* cooes to mourn his Fate.
Oh, sweet Musician, thou dost far excel
The soothing Song of pleasing *Philomel!*
Sweet is her Song, but in few Notes confin'd;
But thine, thou *Mimic* of the feath'ry Kind,
Runs thro' all Notes! – *Thou* only know'st them *All*,
At once the *Copy, – and th' Original.*

THE CALL OF TWO BIRDS

The sea dark,
The call of the teal
Dimly white.

The cuckoo –
Its call stretching
Over the water.

TRANSLATED BY GEOFFREY BOWNAS AND
ANTHONY THWAITE

THE OVEN BIRD

There is a singer everyone has heard,
Loud, a mid-summer and a mid-wood bird,
Who makes the solid tree trunks sound again.
He says that leaves are old and that for flowers
Mid-summer is to spring as one to ten.
He says the early petal-fall is past
When pear and cherry bloom went down in showers
On sunny days a moment overcast;
And comes that other fall we name the fall.
He says the highway dust is over all.
The bird would cease and be as other birds
But that he knows in singing not to sing.
The question that he frames in all but words
Is what to make of a diminished thing.

THE DARKLING THRUSH

I leant upon a coppice gate
    When Frost was spectre-gray,
And Winter's dregs made desolate
    The weakening eye of day.
The tangled bine-stems scored the sky
    Like strings of broken lyres,
And all mankind that haunted nigh
    Had sought their household fires.

The land's sharp features seemed to be
    The Century's corpse outleant,
His crypt the cloudy canopy,
    The wind his death-lament.
The ancient pulse of germ and birth
    Was shrunken hard and dry,
And every spirit upon earth
    Seemed fervourless as I.

At once a voice arose among
 The bleak twigs overhead
In a full-hearted evensong
 Of joy illimited;
An aged thrush, frail, gaunt, and small,
 In blast-beruffled plume,
Had chosen thus to fling his soul
 Upon the growing gloom.

So little cause for carolings
 Of such ecstatic sound
Was written on terrestrial things
 Afar or nigh around,
That I could think there trembled through
 His happy good-night air
Some blessed Hope, whereof he knew
 And I was unaware.

HUMMING-BIRD

I can imagine, in some otherworld
Primeval-dumb, far back
In that most awful stillness, that only gasped and
    hummed,
Humming-birds raced down the avenues.

Before anything had a soul,
While life was a heave of Matter, half inanimate,
This little bit chipped off in brilliance
And went whizzing through the slow, vast, succulent
    stems.

I believe there were no flowers then,
In the world where the humming-bird flashed ahead of
    creation.
I believe he pierced the slow vegetable veins with his
    long beak.

Probably he was big
As mosses, and little lizards, they say, were once big.
Probably he was a jabbing, terrifying monster.

We look at him through the wrong end of the long
    telescope of Time,
Luckily for us.

THE HUMMING BIRD
from 'A Journey from Patapsko to Annapolis'

My *Ear* thus charm'd, mine *Eye* with Pleasure sees,
Hov'ring about the Flow'rs, th'industrious *Bees.*
Like them in Size, the *Humming-Bird* I view,
Like them, *He* sucks his Food, the Honey-Dew,
With nimble Tongue, and Beak of jetty Hue.
He takes with rapid Whirl his noisy Flight,
His gemmy Plumage strikes the Gazer's Sight;
And as he moves his ever-flutt'ring Wings,
Ten thousand Colours he around him flings.
Now I behold the Em'rald's vivid Green,
Now scarlet, now a purple Die is seen;
In brightest Blue, his Breast *He* now arrays,
Then strait his Plumes emit a golden Blaze.
Thus whirring round he flies, and varying still,
He mocks the *Poet*'s and the *Painter*'s Skill;
Who may forever strive with fruitless Pains,
To catch and fix those beauteous changeful Stains;
While Scarlet now, and now the Purple shines,
And Gold, to Blue its transient Gloss resigns.
Each quits, and quickly each resumes its Place,
And ever-varying Dies each other chase.
Smallest of Birds, what Beauties shine in thee!
A living *Rainbow* on thy Breast I see.

Oh had that *Bard* in whose heart-pleasing Lines,
The *Phoenix* in a Blaze of Glory shines,
Beheld those Wonders which are shewn in Thee,
That Bird had lost his Immortality!
Thou in His Verse hadst stretch'd thy flutt'ring Wing
Above all other Birds, – their beauteous King.

LITTLE BIRDS OF THE NIGHT

Little birds of the night
Aye, they have much to tell
Perching there in rows
Blinking at me with their serious eyes
Recounting of flowers they have seen and loved
Of meadows and groves of the distance
And pale sands at the foot of the sea
And breezes that fly in the leaves.
They are vast in experience
These little birds that come in the night.

THE NIBBLERS

THE RAT

The rat is the concisest tenant.
He pays no rent, –
Repudiates the obligation,
On schemes intent.

Balking our wit
To sound or circumvent,
Hate cannot harm
A foe so reticent.

Neither decree
Prohibits him,
Lawful as
Equilibrium.

THE RATS

In the yard the autumn moon shines white,
The roof-edge drops fantastic shadows;
A silence dwells in the empty windows
From which the rats now quietly plunge

And flit about, squeaking, here and there;
A grayish misty exhalation
From the outhouse sniffs after them,
Spectral moonlight trembling through it.

And the rats brawl avidly as if mad
Filling up the house and barn-loft
Already full of grain and fruit.
Icy winds whimper in the yard.

80   GEORG TRAKL
    TRANSLATED BY JOHN HOLLANDER

THE SOUND OF A RAT

Scampering over saucers –
The sound of a rat.
Cold, cold.

YOSA BUSON
TRANSLATED BY GEOFFREY BOWNAS
AND ANTHONY THWAITE

TO A MOUSE, ON TURNING HER UP IN HER NEST, WITH THE PLOUGH, NOVEMBER, 1785.

Wee, sleeket, cowran, tim'rous *beastie*,
O, what a panic 's in thy breastie!
Thou need na start awa sae hasty,
        Wi' bickering brattle!
I wad be laith to rin an' chase thee,
        Wi' murd'ring *pattle!*

I'm truly sorry Man's dominion
Has broken Nature's social union,
An' justifies that ill opinion,
        Which makes thee startle,
At me, thy poor, earth-born companion,
        An' *fellow-mortal!*

I doubt na, whyles, but thou may *thieve*;
What then? poor beastie, thou maun live!
A *daimen-icker* in a *thrave*
        'S a sma' request:
I'll get a blessin wi' the lave,
        An' never miss 't!

Thy wee-bit *housie,* too, in ruin!
It's silly wa's the win's are strewin!
An' naething, now, to big a new ane,
   O' foggage green!
An' bleak *December's winds* ensuin,
   Baith snell an' keen!

Thou saw the fields laid bare an' wast,
An' weary *Winter* comin fast,
An' cozie here, beneath the blast,
   Thou thought to dwell,
Till crash! the cruel *coulter* past
   Out thro' thy cell.

That wee-bit heap o' leaves an' stibble,
Has cost thee monie a weary nibble!
Now thou 's turn'd out, for a' thy trouble,
   But house or hald,
To thole the Winter's *sleety dribble,*
   An' *cranreuch* cauld!

But Mousie, thou art no thy-lane,
In proving *foresight* may be vain:
The best laid schemes o' *Mice* an' *Men*,
        Gang aft agley,
An' lea'e us nought but grief an' pain,
        For promis'd joy!

Still, thou art blest, compar'd wi' *me!*
The *present* only toucheth thee:
But Och! I *backward* cast my e'e,
        On prospects drear!
An' *forward*, tho' I canna *see*,
        I *guess* an' *fear!*

THE BAT

The bat is dun with wrinkled wings
    Like fallow article,
And not a song pervades his lips,
    Or none perceptible.

His small umbrella, quaintly halved,
    Describing in the air
An arc alike inscrutable, –
    Elate philosopher!

Deputed from what firmament
    Of what astute abode,
Empowered with what malevolence
    Auspiciously withheld.

To his adroit Creator
    Ascribe no less the praise;
Beneficent, believe me,
    His eccentricities.

BAT

At evening, sitting on this terrace,
When the sun from the west, beyond Pisa, beyond the
     mountains of Carrara
Departs, and the world is taken by surprise ...

When the tired flower of Florence is in gloom beneath
     the glowing
Brown hills surrounding ...

When under the arches of the Ponte Vecchio
A green light enters against stream, flush from the
     west,
Against the current of obscure Arno ...

Look up, and you see things flying
Between the day and the night;
Swallows with spools of dark thread sewing the
     shadows together.

A circle swoop, and a quick parabola under the bridge
     arches
Where light pushes through;
A sudden turning upon itself of a thing in the air.
A dip to the water.

And you think:
"The swallows are flying so late!"

Swallows?

Dark air-life looping
Yet missing the pure loop ...
A twitch, a twitter, an elastic shudder in flight
And serrated wings against the sky,
Like a glove, a black glove thrown up at the light,
And falling back.

Never swallows!
Bats!
The swallows are gone.

At a wavering instant the swallows give way to bats
By the Ponte Vecchio ...
Changing guard.

Bats, and an uneasy creeping in one's scalp
As the bats swoop overhead!
Flying madly.

Pipistrello!
Black piper on an infinitesimal pipe.

Little lumps that fly in air and have voices indefinite,
    wildly vindictive;

Wings like bits of umbrella.

Bats!

Creatures that hang themselves up like an old rag, to
    sleep;
And disgustingly upside down.
Hanging upside down like rows of disgusting old rags
And grinning in their sleep.
Bats!

In China the bat is symbol of happiness.

Not for me!

TO A SQUIRREL
AT KYLE-NA-NO

Come play with me;
Why should you run
Through the shaking tree
As though I'd a gun
To strike you dead?
When all I would do
Is to scratch your head
And let you go.

MY PET HARE
from The Task, III

Well – one at least is safe. One shelter'd hare
Has never heard the sanguinary yell
Of cruel man, exulting in her woes.
Innocent partner of my peaceful home,
Whom ten long years' experience of my care
Has made at last familiar; she has lost
Much of her vigilant instinctive dread,
Not needful here, beneath a roof like mine.
Yes – thou mayst eat thy bread, and lick the hand
That feeds thee; thou mayst frolic on the floor
At evening, and at night retire secure
To thy straw couch, and slumber unalarm'd;
For I have gain'd thy confidence, have pledged
All that is human in me, to protect
Thine unsuspecting gratitude and love.
If I survive thee, I will dig thy grave;
And, when I place thee in it, sighing say,
I knew at least one hare that had a friend.

THE HUNTED HARE
from Venus and Adonis

And when thou hast on foot the purblind hare,
  Mark the poor wretch, to overshoot his troubles
How he outruns the wind, and with what care
  He cranks and crosses with a thousand doubles:
    The many musits through the which he goes
    Are like a labyrinth to amaze his foes.

Sometime he runs among a flock of sheep,
  To make the cunning hounds mistake their smell,
And sometime where earth-delving conies keep,
  To stop the loud pursuers in their yell,
    And sometime sorteth with a herd of deer;
    Danger deviseth shifts; wit waits on fear:

For there his smell with others being mingled,
  The hot scent-snuffing hounds are driven to doubt,
Ceasing their clamorous cry till they have singled
  With much ado the cold fault cleanly out;
    Then do they spend their mouths: Echo replies,
    As if another chase were in the skies.

By this, poor Wat, far off upon a hill,
   Stands on his hinder legs with listening ear,
To hearken if his foes pursue him still:
   Anon their loud alarums he doth hear;
     And now his grief may be compared well
     To one sore sick that hears the passing-bell.

Then shalt thou see the dew-bedabbled wretch
   Turn, and return, indenting with the way;
Each envious briar his weary legs doth scratch,
   Each shadow makes him stop, each murmur stay:
     For misery is trodden on by many,
     And being low never relieved by any.

THE HUNTED
AND THEIR
HUNTERS

A DOE AT EVENING

As I went through the marshes
a doe sprang out of the corn
and flashed up the hill-side
leaving her fawn.

On the sky-line
she moved round to watch,
she pricked a fine black blotch
on the sky.

I looked at her
and felt her watching;
I became a strange being.
Still, I had my right to be there with her.

Her nimble shadow trotting
along the sky-line, she
put back her fine, level-balanced head.
And I knew her.

Ah yes, being male, is not my head hard-balanced,
    antlered?
Are not my haunches light?
Has she not fled on the same wind with me?
Does not my fear cover her fear?

D. H. LAWRENCE

95

THE FALLOW DEER
AT THE LONELY HOUSE

One without looks in to-night
    Through the curtain-chink
From the sheet of glistening white;
One without looks in to-night
    As we sit and think
    By the fender-brink.

We do not discern those eyes
    Watching in the snow;
Lit by lamps of rosy dyes
We do not discern those eyes
    Wondering, aglow,
    Fourfooted, tiptoe.

CARIBOU

Far, far southward, the forest is white, not merely
As snow of no blemish, but whiter than ice yet sharing
The mystic and blue-tinged, tangential moonlight,
Which in unshadowed vastness breathes northward.
Such great space must once
Have been a lake, now, long ages, ice-solid.

Shadows shift from the whiteness of forest, small
As they move on the verge of moon-shaven distance.
    They grow clear,
As binoculars find the hairline adjustment.
They seem to drift from the purity of forest.
Single, snow-dusted above, each shadow appears, each
Slowly detached from the white anonymity
Of forest, each hulk
Lurching, each lifted leg leaving a blackness as though
Of a broken snowshoe partly withdrawn. We know
That the beast's foot spreads like a snowshoe to
    support
That weight, that bench-kneed awkwardness.

The heads heave and sway. It must be with spittle
That jaws are ice-bearded. The shoulders
Lumber on forward, as though only the bones could,
    inwardly,

Guess destination. The antlers,
Blunted and awkward, are carved by some primitive
        craftsman.

We do not know on what errand they are bent, to
What mission committed. It is a world that
They live in, and it is their life.
They move through the world and breathe destiny.
Their destiny is as bright as crystal, as pure
As a dream of zero. Their destiny
Must resemble happiness even though
They do not know that name.

I lay the binoculars on the lap of the biologist. He
Studies distance. The co-pilot studies a map. He
        glances at
A compass. At mysterious dials. I drink coffee.
        Courteously,
The binoculars come back to me.

I have lost the spot. I find only blankness.

                                        But
They must have been going somewhere.

THE GAZELLE
Gazella Dorcas

Enchanted thing: how can two chosen words
ever attain the harmony of pure rhyme
that pulses through you as your body stirs?
Out of your forehead branch and lyre climb,

and all your features pass in simile, through
the songs of love whose words, as light as rose-
petals, rest on the face of someone who
has put his book away and shut his eyes:

to see you: tensed, as if each leg were a gun
loaded with leaps, but not fired while your neck
holds your head still, listening: as when,

while swimming in some isolated place,
a girl hears leaves rustle, and turns to look:
the forest pool reflected in her face.

RAINER MARIA RILKE
TRANSLATED BY STEPHEN MITCHELL

THE HOWLING OF WOLVES

Is without world.

What are they dragging up and out on their long
      leashes of sound
That dissolve in the mid-air silence?

Then crying of a baby, in this forest of starving
      silences,
Brings the wolves running.
Tuning of a violin, in this forest delicate as an owl's ear,
Brings the wolves running – brings the steel traps
      clashing and slavering,
The steel furred to keep it from cracking in the cold,
The eyes that never learn how it has come about
That they must live like this,

That they must live

Innocence crept into minerals.

The wind sweeps through and the hunched wolf
      shivers.
It howls you cannot say whether out of agony or joy.

The earth is under its tongue,
A dead weight of darkness, trying to see through its
    eyes.
The wolf is living for the earth.
But the wolf is small, it comprehends little.

It goes to and fro, trailing its haunches and
    whimpering horribly.
It must feed its fur.

The night snows stars and the earth creaks.

HUNTING-SONG OF THE SEEONEE PACK
from The Jungle Book

As the dawn was breaking the Sambhur belled –
    Once, twice and again!
And a doe leaped up, and a doe leaped up
From the pond in the wood where the wild deer sup.
This I, scouting alone, beheld,
    Once, twice and again!

As the dawn was breaking the Sambhur belled –
    Once, twice and again!
And a wolf stole back, and a wolf stole back
To carry the word to the waiting pack,
And we sought and we found and we bayed on his
    track
    Once, twice and again!

As the dawn was breaking the Wolf-Pack yelled
    Once, twice and again!
Feet in the jungle that leave no mark!
Eyes that can see in the dark – the dark!
Tongue – give tongue to it! Hark! O Hark!
    Once, twice and again!

THE PANTHER
In the Jardin des Plantes, Paris

His vision, from the constantly passing bars,
has grown so weary that it cannot hold
anything else. It seems to him there are
a thousand bars; and behind the bars, no world.

As he paces in cramped circles, over and over,
the movement of his powerful soft strides
is like a ritual dance around a center
in which a mighty will stands paralyzed.

Only at times, the curtain of the pupils
lifts, quietly –. An image enters in,
rushes down through the tensed, arrested muscles,
plunges into the heart and is gone.

RAINER MARIA RILKE
TRANSLATED BY STEPHEN MITCHELL

THE SNOW-LEOPARD

His pads furring the scarp's rime,
Weightless in greys and ecru, gliding
Invisibly, incuriously
As the crystals of the cirri wandering
A mile below his absent eyes,
The leopard gazes at the caravan.
The yaks groaning with tea, the burlaps
Lapping and lapping each stunned universe
That gasps like a kettle for its thinning life
Are pools in the interminable abyss
That ranges up through ice, through air, to night.
Raiders of the unminding element,
The last cold capillaries of their kind,
They move so slowly they are motionless
To any eye less stubborn than a man's. . . .
From the implacable jumble of the blocks
The grains dance icily, a scouring plume,
Into the breath, sustaining, unsustainable,
They trade to that last stillness for their death.
They sense with misunderstanding horror, with desire,
Behind the world their blood sets up in mist
The brute and geometrical necessity:
The leopard waving with a grating purr
His six-foot tail; the leopard, who looks sleepily –
Cold, fugitive, secure – at all that he knows,
At all that he is: the heart of heartlessness.

THE BEAR

In the huge, wide-open, sleeping eye of the mountain
The bear is the gleam in the pupil
Ready to awake
And instantly focus.

The bear is glueing
Beginning to end
With glue from people's bones
In his sleep.

The bear is digging
In his sleep
Through the wall of the Universe
With a man's femur.

The bear is a well
Too deep to glitter
Where your shout
Is being digested.

The bear is a river
Where people bending to drink
See their dead selves.

The bear sleeps
In a kingdom of walls
In a web of rivers.

He is the ferryman
To dead land.

His price is everything.

ROAD-SONG OF THE *BANDAR-LOG*
from The Jungle Book

Here we go in a flung festoon,
Half-way up to the jealous moon!
Don't you envy our pranceful bands?
Don't you wish you had extra hands?
Wouldn't you like if your tails were – *so* –
Curved in the shape of a Cupid's bow?
　　Now you're angry, but – never mind,
　　Brother, thy tail hangs down behind!

Here we sit in a branchy row,
Thinking of beautiful things we know;
Dreaming of deeds that we mean to do,
All complete, in a minute or two –
Something noble and grand and good,
Won by merely wishing we could.
　　Now we're going to – never mind,
　　Brother, thy tail hangs down behind!

All the talk we ever have heard
Uttered by bat or beast or bird –
Hide or fin or scale or feather –
Jabber it quickly and all together!
Excellent! Wonderful! Once again!
Now we are talking just like men.

Let's pretend we are ... Never mind!
Brother, thy tail hangs down behind!
This is the way of the Monkey-kind!

Then join our leaping lines that scumfish through the pines,
That rocket by where, light and high, the wild-grape swings.
By the rubbish in our wake, and the noble noise we make,
Be sure — be sure, we're going to do some splendid things!

TO A GIRAFFE

If it is unpermissible, in fact fatal
to be personal and undesirable

to be literal – detrimental as well
if the eye is not innocent – does it mean that

one can live only on top leaves that are small
reachable only by a beast that is tall? –

of which the giraffe is the best example –
the unconversational animal.

When plagued by the psychological,
a creature can be unbearable

that could have been irresistible;
or to be exact, exceptional

since less conversational
than some emotionally-tied-in-knots animal.

    After all
consolations of the metaphysical
can be profound. In Homer, existence

   is flawed; transcendence, conditional;
"the journey from sin to redemption, perpetual."

THE ELEPHANT

I will remember what I was. I am sick of rope and chain –
   I will remember my old strength and all my
      forest-affairs.
I will not sell my back to man for a bundle of
      sugar-cane.
   I will go out to my own kind, and the wood-folk in
      their lairs.

I will go out until the day, until the morning break,
   Out to the winds' untainted kiss, the waters' clean
      caress.
I will forget my ankle-ring and snap my picket-stake.
   I will revisit my lost loves, and playmates
      masterless!

SOME WINGED
PREDATORS

THE EAGLE

He clasps the crag with crooked hands;
Close to the sun in lonely lands,
Ringed with the azure world, he stands.

The wrinkled sea beneath him crawls;
He watches from his mountain walls,
And like a thunderbolt he falls.

ALFRED, LORD TENNYSON

THE DALLIANCE OF THE EAGLES

Skirting the river road, (my forenoon walk, my rest,)
Skyward in air a sudden muffled sound, the dalliance of
    the eagles,
The rushing amorous contact high in space together,
The clinching interlocking claws, a living, fierce,
    gyrating wheel,
Four beating wings, two beaks, a swirling mass tight
    grappling,
In tumbling turning clustering loops, straight
    downward falling,
Till o'er the river pois'd, the twain yet one, a moment's
    lull,
A motionless still balance in the air, then parting,
    talons loosing,
Upward again on slow-firm pinions slanting, their
    separate diverse flight,
She hers, he his, pursuing.

THE CARRION CROW

Old Adam, the carrion crow,
    The old crow of Cairo;
He sat in the shower, and let it flow
      Under his tail and over his crest;
        And through every feather
        Leaked the wet weather;
      And the bough swung under his nest;
For his beak it was heavy with marrow.
      Is that the wind dying? Oh no;
      It's only two devils, that blow
        Through a murderer's bones, to and fro,
          In the ghosts' moonshine.

Ho! Eve, my grey carrion wife,
    When we have supped on kings' marrow,
Where shall we drink and make merry our life?
      Our nest it is queen Cleopatra's skull,
        'Tis cloven and cracked,
        And battered and hacked,
      But with tears of blue eyes it is full:
Let us drink then, my raven of Cairo.
      Is that the wind dying? O no;
      It's only two devils, that blow
        Through a murderer's bones, to and fro,
          In the ghosts' moonshine.

THE MAN-OF-WAR HAWK

Yon black man-of-war hawk that wheels in the light
O'er the black ship's white sky-s'l, sunned cloud to the
    sight,
Have we low-flyers wings to ascend to his height?

No arrow can reach him; nor thought can attain
To the placid supreme in the sweep of his reign.

TO THE MAN-OF-WAR BIRD

Thou who hast slept all night upon the storm,
Waking renew'd on thy prodigious pinions,
(Burst the wild storm? above it thou ascended'st,
And rested on the sky, thy slave that cradled thee,)
Now a blue point, far, far in heaven floating,
As to the light emerging here on deck I watch thee,
(Myself a speck, a point on the world's floating vast.)

Far, far at sea,
After the night's fierce drifts have strewn the shore
      with wrecks,
With re-appearing day as now so happy and serene,
The rosy and elastic dawn, the flashing sun,
The limpid spread of air cerulean,
Thou also re-appearest.

Thou born to match the gale, (thou art all wings,)
To cope with heaven and earth and sea and hurricane,
Thou ship of air that never furl'st thy sails,
Days, even weeks untired and onward, through spaces,
      realms gyrating,
At dusk that look'st on Senegal, at morn America,
That sport'st amid the lightning-flash and thunder-cloud,
In them, in thy experiences, had'st thou my soul,
What joys! what joys were thine!

OWLS

Under black yews that protect them
    the owls perch in a row
like alien gods whose red eyes
    glitter. They meditate.

Petrified, they will perch there till
    the melancholy hour
when the slanting sun is ousted,
    and darkness settles down.

From their posture, the wise
learn to shun, in this world at least,
    motion and commotion;

impassioned by passing shadows,
    man will always be scourged
for trying to change his place.

CHARLES BAUDELAIRE
TRANSLATED BY RICHARD HOWARD

THE OWL

Downhill I came, hungry, and yet not starved;
Cold, yet had heat within me that was proof
Against the North wind; tired, yet so that rest
Had seemed the sweetest thing under a roof.

Then at the inn I had food, fire, and rest,
Knowing how hungry, cold, and tired was I.
All of the night was quite barred out except
An owl's cry, a most melancholy cry

Shaken out long and clear upon the hill,
No merry note, nor cause of merriment,
But one telling me plain what I escaped
And others could not, that night, as in I went.

And salted was my food, and my repose,
Salted and sobered, too, by the bird's voice
Speaking for all who lay under the stars,
Soldiers and poor, unable to rejoice.

EDWARD THOMAS   119

EVENING HAWK

From plane of light to plane, wings dipping through
Geometries and orchids that the sunset builds,
Out of the peak's black angularity of shadow, riding
The last tumultuous avalanche of
Light above pines and the guttural gorge,
The hawk comes.

           His wing
Scythes down another day, his motion
Is that of the honed steel-edge, we hear
The crashless fall of stalks of Time.

The head of each stalk is heavy with the gold of our
     error.

Look! Look! he is climbing the last light
Who knows neither Time nor error, and under
Whose eye, unforgiving, the world, unforgiven, swings
Into shadow.

                    Long now,
The last thrush is still, the last bat
Now cruises in his sharp hieroglyphics. His wisdom
Is ancient, too, and immense. The star
Is steady, like Plato, over the mountain.

If there were no wind we might, we think, hear
The earth grind on its axis, or history
Drip in darkness like a leaking pipe in the cellar.

TAMER AND HAWK

I thought I was so tough,
But gentled at your hands
Cannot be quick enough
To fly for you and show
That when I go I go
At your commands.

Even in flight above
I am no longer free:
You seeled me with your love,
I am blind to other birds –
The habit of your words
Has hooded me.

As formerly, I wheel
I hover and I twist,
But only want the feel
In my possessive thought,
Of catcher and of caught
Upon your wrist.

You but half-civilize,
Taming me in this way.
Through having only eyes
For you I fear to losé,
I lose to keep, and choose
Tamer as prey.

TINY,
UNWELCOME
GUESTS

THE FLEA

Mark but this flea, and mark in this,
How little that which thou deny'st me is;
Me it sucked first, and now sucks thee,
And in this flea, our two bloods mingled be;
Confess it, this cannot be said
A sin, or shame, or loss of maidenhead,
   Yet this enjoys before it woo,
    And pampered swells with one blood made of two,
    And this, alas, is more than we would do.

Oh stay, three lives in one flea spare,
Where we almost, nay more than married are.
This flea is you and I, and this
Our marriage bed, and marriage temple is;
Though parents grudge, and you, we are met,
And cloistered in these living walls of jet.
   Though use make you apt to kill me,
    Let not to this, self murder added be,
    And sacrilege, three sins in killing three.

Cruel and sudden, hast thou since
Purpled thy nail, in blood of innocence?
In what could this flea guilty be,
Except in that drop which it sucked from thee?
Yet thou triumph'st, and say'st that thou
Find'st not thyself nor me the weaker now;
   'Tis true, then learn how false, fears be;
   Just so much honour, when thou yield'st to me,
   Will waste, as this flea's death took life from thee.

THE BLUE-FLY

Five summer days, five summer nights,
The ignorant, loutist, giddy blue-fly
Hung without motion on the cling peach,
Humming occasionally: 'O my love, my fair one!'
    As in the *Canticles*.

Magnified one thousand times, the insect
Looks farcically human; laugh if you will!
Bald head, stage-fairy wings, blear eyes,
A caved-in chest, hairy black mandibles,
    Long spindly thighs.

The crime was detected on the sixth day.
What then could be said or done? By anyone?
It would have been vindictive, mean and what-not
To swat that fly for being a blue-fly,
    For debauch of a peach.

Is it fair, either, to bring a microscope
To bear on the case, even in search of truth?
Nature, doubtless, has some compelling cause
To glut the carriers of her epidemics –
    Nor did the peach complain.

ROBERT GRAVES

SWARMING MOSQUITOES

The sun has set, the moon is in darkness;
now the mosquitoes fly forth from cracked walls.
They swarm in the void with a thunderous hum,
dance in the courtyard like a veil of mist.
The spider's web is uselessly spread;
the mantis can't slash them with his ax.
The vicious scorpion helps them in their mischief
and freely stings with his belly's poison;
because he has no wings to use,
he patters and scratches up the darkened wall.
Noblemen reside in lordly mansions,
silken nets encircling their beds.
Would that in such homes as these
the mosquitoes flaunted their lance-like beaks!
Instead they frequent the poor and humble
with no compassion for their gauntness.
Suckers sharp, they race to the attack;
drinking blood, they seek self-increase.
The bat flits back and forth in vain;
he cannot kill or capture them.
The chirping cicada, sated with wind and dew,
shamelessly goes on sipping more.
– This hum and buzz can't last much longer:
The east will soon be bright.

TRANSLATED BY JONATHAN CHAVES

TO A LOUSE, ON SEEING ONE ON A LADY'S BONNET AT CHURCH

Ha! whare ye gaun, ye crowlan ferlie!
Your impudence protects you sairly:
I canna say but ye strunt rarely,
   Owre *gawze* and *lace*;
Tho' faith, I fear ye dine but sparely,
   On sic a place.

Ye ugly, creepan, blastet wonner,
Detested, shunn'd, by saunt an' sinner,
How daur ye set your fit upon her,
   Sae fine a *Lady*!
Gae somewhere else and seek your dinner,
   On some poor body.

Swith, in some beggar's haffet squattle;
There ye may creep, and sprawl, and sprattle,
Wi' ither kindred, jumping cattle,
   In shoals and nations;
Whare *horn* nor *bane* ne'er daur unsettle,
   Your thick plantations.

Now haud you there, ye're out o' sight,
Below the fatt'rels, snug and tight,
Na faith ye yet! ye'll no be right,
        Till ye've got on it,
The vera tapmost, towrin height
        O' *Miss's bonnet.*

My sooth! right bauld ye set your nose out,
As plump an' gray as onie grozet:
O for some rank, mercurial rozet,
        Or fell, red smeddum,
I'd gie you sic a hearty dose o't,
        Wad dress your droddum!

I wad na been surpriz'd to spy
You on an auld wife's *flainen toy*;
Or aiblins some bit duddie boy,
        On 's *wylecoat*;
But Miss's fine *Lundardi*, fye!
    How daur ye do't?

O *Jenny* dinna toss your head,
An' set your beauties a' abread!
Ye little ken what cursed speed
  The blastie's makin!
Thae *winks* and *finger-ends*, I dread,
  Are notice takin!

O wad some Pow'r the giftie gie us
To see oursels as others see us!
It wad frae monie a blunder free us
  An' foolish notion:
What airs in dress an' gait wad lea'e us,
  And ev'n Devotion!

THE WASP

It was a wasp or an imprudent bee
Against my skin, underneath my shirt,
That stung as I was trying to set it free.
Art is perhaps too long, or life too short.

Ignorant of entomology
I watched it at the crumbs of my dessert,
Numbered its stripes, curious what sort
Of wasp it was, or what tribe of bee,

While bored, aware that it was watched, maybe,
Buzzing, it appeared to pay me court,
And darted in where I could not see
It, against my skin, underneath my shirt,

There in the sweaty twilight next to me
Its amorous antennae to disport,
But always armed. The minute, golden flirt
Stung as I was trying to set it free.

So it escaped, but died eventually,
An event exceeding its desert,
While I, stung as I deserved to be –
But art is perhaps too long, or life too short.

Trivial, scarce worthy of report,
Wonderful the wounds of love should be
Occasion, none the less, for poetry.
Thus deaths, that is the deaths of others, hurt.
                              It was a wasp.

THAT CREEPETH
UPON THE
EARTH

A NARROW FELLOW

A narrow fellow in the grass
Occasionally rides;
You may have met him, – did you not?
His notice sudden is.

The grass divides as with a comb,
A spotted shaft is seen;
And then it closes at your feet
And opens further on.

He likes a boggy acre,
A floor too cool for corn.
Yet when a child, and barefoot,
I more than once at morn,

Have passed, I thought, a whip-lash
Unbraiding in the sun, –
When stooping to secure it,
It wrinkled, and was gone.

Several of nature's people
I know, and they know me;
I feel for them a transport
Of cordiality;

But never met this fellow,
Attended or alone,
Without a tighter breathing,
And zero at the bone.

SNAKE

Close by the creepered wall,
On the cinquefoil's shaggy border,
He takes the sun, and the unwary fly.
The snake is named Disorder.

This garter's all reversed,
Elastic frayed, the yellow stripe
Of species a dirty, bulging seam —
Precision's antitype.

He's a pile of himself!
Too old, too devil-may-care. And yet . . .
That staring eye and wrap-around grin
Unearth a buried debt.

To what? You back away,
Then turn to cultivate some quarter
Of the garden, sulking rows that say
The snake is named Disorder.

TO A SNAIL

If "compression is the first grace of style,"
you have it. Contractility is a virtue
as modesty is a virtue.
It is not the acquisition of any one thing
that is able to adorn,
or the incidental quality that occurs
as a concomitant of something well said,
that we value in style,
but the principle that is hid:
in the absence of feet, "a method of conclusions";
"a knowledge of principles,"
in the curious phenomenon of your occipital horn.

from THE SNAIL

Wise emblem of our politic world,
Sage snail, within thine own self curled;
Instruct me softly to make haste,
Whilst these my feet go slowly fast.
    Compendious snail! thou seem'st to me
Large Euclid's strict epitome;
And in each diagram, dost fling
Thee from the point unto the ring.
A figure now triangular,
An oval now, and now a square,
And then a serpentine dost crawl,
Now a straight line, now crook'd, now all ...
    Thou thine own daughter then, and sire,
That son and mother art entire,
That big still with thyself dost go,
And liv'st an aged embryo;
That like the cubs of India,
Thou from thyself a while dost play;
But frightened with a dog or gun,
In thine own belly thou dost run,
And as thy house was thine own womb,
So thine own womb concludes thy tomb ...

Now hast thou changed thee saint; and made
Thyself a fane that's cupola'd,
And in thy wreathéd cloister thou
Walkest thine own gray friar too;
Strict, and locked up, th'art hood all o'er
And ne'er eliminat'st thy door.
On salads thou dost feed severe,
And 'stead of beads thou drop'st a tear,
And when to rest, each calls the bell,
Thou sleep'st within thy marble cell,
Where in dark contemplation placed,
The sweets of nature thou dost taste;
Who now with time thy days resolve,
And in a jelly thee dissolve
Like a shot star, which doth repair
Upward, and rarefy the air.

SLUG

How I loved one like you when I was little! –
With his stripes of silver and his small house on his
       back,
Making a slow journey around the well-curb.
I longed to be like him, and was,
In my way, close cousin
To the dirt, my knees scrubbing
The gravel, my nose wetter than his.

When I slip, just slightly, in the dark,
I know it isn't a wet leaf,
But you, loose toe from the old life,
The cold slime come into being,
A fat, five-inch appendage
Creeping slowly over the wet grass,
Eating the heart out of my garden.

And you refuse to die decently! –
Flying upward through the knives of my lawnmower
Like pieces of smoked eel or raw oyster,
And I go faster in my rage to get done with it,
Until I'm scraping and scratching at you, on the
       doormat,
The small dead pieces sticking under an instep;

Or, poisoned, dragging a white skein of spittle over a
     path –
Beautiful, in its way, like quicksilver –
You shrink to something less,
A rain-drenched fly or spider.

I'm sure I've been a toad, one time or another.
With bats, weasels, worms – I rejoice in the kinship.
Even the caterpillar I can love, and the various vermin.
But as for you, most odious –
Would Blake call you holy?

THE TOAD

A song in a windless night ...
– The moon plates in metal bright
The cut-out images of dark green.

... A song; sudden as an echo, quick,
Buried, there, under the thick
Clump. It stops. Come, it's there, unseen ...

– A toad! – There in shadow. – Why this terror
Near me, your faithful soldier? – Spring! –
Look at him, poet clipped, no wing,
Nightingale of the mud ... – Horror! –

... – He sings. – Horror!! – Horror! But why?
Don't you see that eye of light, his own?
No: he goes, chilled, beneath his stone.
Good-night. That toad you heard is I.

TRISTAN CORBIÈRE

TRANSLATED BY VERNON WATKINS

THE TOAD

The bluish twilight sinks with dripping dews,
Dragging behind its broad, rose-golden fringes.
Lone poplars stand out black on soft pale hues;
A tender birch dissolves to mist-gray tinges,
And apples roll like skulls toward the furrows.
The leaves, like crackling embers, fade to brown,
While ghostly lamps peer from a distant town.
White meadow fog brews beasts within their burrows.

I am the toad.
I love the stars of night.
The coals of sunset, evening's ruddy lode,
Smoulder in purple ponds, barely alight.
Beneath the rainbarrel's sodden wood
I crouch, low, fat, and wise.
My painful moon-eyes wait and brood
To view the sun's demise.

I am the toad,
And whispering night is my abode.
A slender flutist stirs
And sings in swaying reeds and sedge.
A velvet violinist whirrs
And fiddles at the field's edge.
I listen, silent, from my soggy seat.
Then, pushing with my fingery feet,

Beneath the rotten planks I creep.
Out of the morass, inch by inch I wind,
Like a thought that, buried deep,
Emerges from a muddled mind.
Through weeds I hop and over gravel,
A dark and humble sense.
Over dew-soaked leaves I travel
Toward the black-green ivy by the fence.

I breathe and swim
Upon a peaceful deep.
And from the garden's rim,
With modest voice I peep
Amid the feathered night, and rest
Defenseless. So be cruel –
Come kill me! Though to you I'm but a pest:
I am the toad, and wear a precious jewel ...

GERTRUD KOLMAR
TRANSLATED BY HENRY A. SMITH

ON A TOAD

Its savage eyes, at whom do they glare?
Its whitish belly swells in vain.
Just take care not to worry the centipede,
A hungry snake will never let you go free.

TRANSLATED BY IRVING Y. LO

SEEING THE FROG

Seeing the frog
and on its back
embroidery like eyes,
I felt it "see" me
also as shadow
in disguise.

Lengthening
without motion
carefully my hand
lowered a socket –
and unclosed a pond.

Memory handed me
a frog,
pulse under thumb:
how to hold
a loose thing tight,
yet not lame.

The jerk, the
narrow hips' escape
happened again.
I felt the chill
embossment and
the ticking chin.

Before the splash
a hand spread
in whole design,
tan and shadow-
patched, the warts
of water mine!

TO A CHAMELEON

Hid by the august foliage and fruit of the grape-vine
   twine
      your anatomy
         round the pruned and polished stem,
           Chameleon.
           Fire laid upon
         an emerald as long as
       the Dark King's massy
     one,
could not snap the spectrum up for food as you have
                           done.

CATERPILLAR

How soft a Caterpillar steps –
I find one on my Hand
From such a velvet world it comes
Such plushes at command
Its soundless travels just arrest
My slow – terrestrial eye
Intent upon its own career
What use has it for me –

THE SILKWORM

The beams of April, ere it goes,
A worm, scarce visible, disclose;
All winter long content to dwell
The tenant of his native shell.
The same prolific season gives
The sustenance by which he lives,
The mulberry leaf, a simple store,
That serves him – till he needs no more!
For, his dimensions once complete,
Thenceforth none ever sees him eat;
Though till his growing time be past
Scarce ever is he seen to fast.
That hour arrived, his work begins.
He spins and weaves, and weaves and spins;
Till circle upon circle wound
Careless around him and around,
Conceals him with a veil, though slight,
Impervious to the keenest sight.
Thus self-inclosed as in a cask,
At length he finishes his task;
And, though a worm when he was lost,
Or caterpillar at the most,
When next we see him, wings he wears,
And in papilio pomp appears;
Becomes oviparous; supplies

With future worms and future flies
The next ensuing year – and dies!
Well were it for the world, if all
Who creep about this earthly ball,
Though shorter lived than most he be,
Were useful in their kind as he.

TRANSLATED BY WILLIAM COWPER

A CROCODILE

Hard by the lilied Nile I saw
A duskish river-dragon stretched along,
The brown habergeon of his limbs enamelled
With sanguine alamandines and rainy pearl:
And on his back there lay a young one sleeping,
No bigger than a mouse; with eyes like beads,
And a small fragment of its speckled egg
Remaining on its harmless, pulpy snout;
A thing to laugh at, as it gaped to catch
The baulking merry flies. In the iron jaws
Of the great devil-beast, like a pale soul
Fluttering in rocky hell, lightsomely flew
A snowy trochilus, with roseate beak
Tearing the hairy leeches from his throat.

THE LOVES OF THE TORTOISE
from Halieutica

Justly might Female *Tortoises* complain,
To whom Enjoyment is the greatest Pain,
They dread the Tryal, and foreboding hate
The growing Passion of the cruel Mate.
He amorous pursues, They conscious fly
Joyless Caresses, and resolv'd deny.
Since partial Heav'n has thus restrain'd the Bliss,
The Males they welcome with a closer Kiss,
Bite angry, and reluctant Hate declare.
The *Tortoise*-Courtship is a State of War.

Eager they fight, but with unlike Design,
Males to obtain, and Females to decline.
The conflict lasts, till these by Strength o'ercome
All sorrowing yield to the resistless Doom.
Not like a Bride, but pensive Captive, led
To the loath'd Duties of an hated Bed.
The *Seal*, and *Tortoise* copulate behind
Like Earth-bred Dogs, and are not soon disjoyn'd;
But secret Ties the passive Couple bind.

     TRANSLATED BY WILLIAM DIAPER

TORTOISE GALLANTRY

Making his advances
He does not look at her, nor sniff at her,
No, not even sniff at her, his nose is blank.

Only he senses the vulnerable folds of skin
That work beneath her while she sprawls along
In her ungainly pace,
Her folds of skin that work and row
Beneath the earth-soiled hovel in which she moves.

And so he strains beneath her housey walls
And catches her trouser-legs in his beak
Suddenly, or her skinny limb,
And strange and grimly drags at her
Like a dog,
Only agelessly silent, with a reptile's awful persistency.

Grim, gruesome gallantry, to which he is doomed.
Dragged out of an eternity of silent isolation
And doomed to partiality, partial being,
Ache, and want of being,
Want,
Self-exposure, hard humiliation, need to add himself on
    to her.

Born to walk alone,
Fore-runner,
Now suddenly distracted into this mazy side-track,
This awkward, harrowing pursuit,
This grim necessity from within.

Does she know
As she moves eternally slowly away?
Or is he driven against her with a bang, like a bird
    flying in the dark against a window,
All knowledgeless?

The awful concussion,
And the still more awful need to persist, to follow,
    follow, continue,

Driven, after æons of pristine, fore-god-like singleness
    and oneness,
At the end of some mysterious, red-hot iron,
Driven away from himself into her tracks,
Forced to crash against her.

Stiff, gallant, irascible, crook-legged reptile,
Little gentleman,
Sorry plight,
We ought to look the other way.

Save that, having come with you so far,
We will go on to the end.

GIANT TORTOISE

I am related to stones
The slow accretion of moss where dirt is wedged
Long waxy hair that can split boulders.
Events are not important.

I live in my bone
Recalling the hour of my death.
It takes more toughness than most have got.
Or a saintliness.

Strength of a certain kind, anyway.
Bald toothless clumsy perhaps
With all the indignity of old age
But age is not important.

There is nothing worth remembering
But the silver glint in the muck
The thickening of great trees
The hard crust getting harder.

WHAT THE WATERS BRING FORTH ABUNDANTLY

THE FISH

In a cool curving world he lies
And ripples with dark ecstasies.
The kind luxurious lapse and steal
Shapes all his universe to feel
And know and be; the clinging stream
Closes his memory, glooms his dream,
Who lips the roots o' the shore, and glides
Superb on unreturning tides.
Those silent waters weave for him
A fluctuant mutable world and dim,
Where wavering masses bulge and gape
Mysterious, and shape to shape
Dies momently through whorl and hollow,
And form and line and solid follow
Solid and line and form to dream
Fantastic down the eternal stream;
An obscure world, a shifting world,
Bulbous, or pulled to thin, or curled,
Or serpentine, or driving arrows,
Or serene slidings, or March narrows.
There slipping wave and shore are one,
And weed and mud. No ray of sun,
But glow to glow fades down the deep
(As dream to unknown dream in sleep);
Shaken translucency illumes

The hyaline of drifting glooms;
The strange soft-handed depth subdues
Drowned colour there, but black to hues,
As death to living, decomposes –
Red darkness of the heart of roses,
Blue brilliant from dead starless skies,
And gold that lies behind the eyes,
The unknown unnameable sightless white
That is the essential flame of night,
Lustreless purple, hooded green,
The myriad hues that lie between
Darkness and darkness! . . .

                And all's one
Gentle, embracing, quiet, dun,
The world he rests in, world he knows,
Perpetual curving. Only – grows
An eddy in that ordered falling,
A knowledge from the gloom, a calling
Weed in the wave, gleam in the mud –
The dark fire leaps along his blood;
Dateless and deathless, blind and still,
The intricate impulse works its will;
His woven world drops back; and he,
Sans providence, sans memory,
Unconscious and directly driven,
Fades to some dank sufficient heaven.

O world of lips, O world of laughter,
Where hope is fleet and thought flies after,
Of lights in the clear night, of cries
That drift along the wave and rise
Thin to the glittering stars above,
You know the hands, the eyes of love!
The strife of limbs, the sightless clinging,
The infinite distance, and the singing
Blown by the wind, a flame of sound,
The gleam, the flowers, and vast around
The horizon, and the heights above –
You know the sigh, the song of love!

But there the night is close, and there
Darkness is cold and strange and bare;
And the secret deeps are whisperless;
And rhythm is all deliciousness;
And joy is in the throbbing tide,
Whose intricate fingers beat and glide
In felt bewildering harmonies
Of trembling touch; and music is
The exquisite knocking of the blood.
Space is no more, under the mud;
His bliss is older than the sun.
Silent and straight the waters run.
The lights, the cries, the willows dim,
And the dark tide are one with him.

THE RED MULLET

The fig flames inward on the bough, and I,
Deep where the great mullet, red, lounges in
Black shadow of the shoal, have come. Where no light
    may

Come, he the great one, like flame, burns, and I
Have met him, eye to eye, the lower jaw horn,
Outthrust, arched down at the corners, merciless as

Genghis, motionless and mogul, and the eye of
The mullet is round, bulging, ringed like a target
In gold, vision is armor, he sees and does not

Forgive. The mullet has looked me in the eye, and
    forgiven
Nothing. At night I fear suffocation, is there
Enough air in the world for us all, therefore I

Swim much, dive deep to develop my lung-case, I am
Familiar with the agony of will in the deep place. Blood
Thickens as oxygen fails. Oh, mullet, thy flame

Burns in the shadow of the black shoal.

THE MALDIVE SHARK

About the Shark, phlegmatical one,
Pale sot of the Maldive sea,
The sleek little pilot-fish, azure and slim,
How alert in attendance be.
From his saw-pit of mouth, from his charnel of maw
They have nothing of harm to dread,
But liquidly glide on his ghastly flank
Or before his Gorgonian head;
Or lurk in the port of serrated teeth
In white triple tiers of glittering gates,
And there find a haven when peril's abroad,
An asylum in jaws of the Fates!

They are friends; and friendly they guide him to prey,
Yet never partake of the treat –
Eyes and brains to the dotard lethargic and dull,
Pale ravener of horrible meat.

HERMAN MELVILLE   169

REMORA

This life is deep and dense
Beyond all seeing, yet one sees, in spite
Of being littler, a degree or two
Further than those one is attracted to.

Pea-brained, myopic, often brutal,
When chosen they have no defense –
A sucking sore there on the belly's pewter –
And where two go could be one's finer sense.

Who now descends from a machine
Plumed with bubbles, death in his right hand?
Lunge, numbskull! One, two, three worlds boil.
Thanks for the lift. There are other fish in the sea.

Still on occasion as by oversight
One lets be taken clinging fast
In heavenly sunshine to the corpse a slight
Tormented self, live, dapper, black-and-white.

THE LOVES OF THE EEL
from Halieutica

Strange the Formation of the *Eely* Race,
That know no Sex, yet love the close Embrace.
Their folded Lengths they round each other twine,
Twist am'rous Knots, and slimy Bodies joyn:
Till the close Strife brings off a frothy Juice,
The Seed that must the wriggling Kind produce.
Regardless They their future Offspring leave,
But porous Sands the spumy Drops receive.
That genial Bed impregnates all the Heap,
And little *Eelets* soon begin to creep.
Half-Fish, Half-Slime they try their doubtful strength,
And slowly trail along their wormy Length.
What great Effects from slender Causes flow!
Congers their Bulk to these Productions owe:
The Forms, which from the frothy Drop began,
Stretch out immense, and eddy all the Main.

THE CRAYFISH

Uncertainty, O my delight
You and I must move along
As crayfish always move in flight,
Backwards, though it may seem wrong.

TRANSLATED BY ROGER SHATTUCK

THE CHAMBERED NAUTILUS

This is the ship of pearl, which, poets feign,
   Sails the unshadowed main, –
   The venturous bark that flings
On the sweet summer wind its purpled wings
In gulfs enchanted, where the siren sings,
   And coral reefs lie bare,
Where the cold sea-maids rise to sun their streaming
     hair.

Its webs of living gauze no more unfurl;
   Wrecked is the ship of pearl!
   And every chambered cell,
Where its dim dreaming life was wont to dwell,
As the frail tenant shaped his growing shell,
   Before thee lies revealed, –
Its irised ceiling rent, its sunless crypt unsealed!

Year after year beheld the silent toil
   That spread his lustrous coil;
   Still, as the spiral grew,
He left the past year's dwelling for the new,
Stole with soft step its shining archway through,
   Built up its idle door,
Stretched in his last-found home, and knew the old no
     more.

Thanks for the heavenly message brought by thee,
    Child of the wandering sea,
    Cast from her lap forlorn!
From thy dead lips a clearer note is born
Than ever Triton blew from wreathèd horn!
    While on mine ear it rings,
Through the deep caves of thought I hear a voice that
    sings: —

Build thee more stately mansions, O my soul,
    As the swift seasons roll!
    Leave thy low-vaulted past!
Let each new temple, nobler than the last,
Shut thee from heaven with a dome more vast,
    Till thou at length art free,
Leaving thine outgrown shell by life's unresting sea!

THE SEA HORSE

This sea horse, errant upon Sargasso weed,
Came on the tiny bladders to these colder shores,
Squirmed from the loaded scallop–dredge, slid
Among the clutter, being swept abruptly from the lairs
Of king-crab, conch and starfish, to collide

With an unassimilatable element. Its tail,
Prehensile, curled strongly round my finger,
A rigid band, harsh for one so very small,
As if its horror of the air had forced an anger
Against my hand, lying limply in the cull

Of broken shells and eel grass. Eyes were blue
Against its shiny black, and flexible armour
Was not crisp and brittle as in the dry
One before me on my table as I write here;
Recalling later the wonders of a world I hardly know.

This strange and amulet fish attracts
As no other, though it is true that man as male
Sheers from the brood-pouched stallion, rejects
A system which might make him also feel
The burdens of motherhood. These defects

In my imagination still cannot destroy
My appreciation of this so unfamiliar stranger,
Which, for a long moment, I held, let lie
Convulsive in my palm, then watched it linger
In reorientation before it twirled away

Upright in the water; dorsal fin as screw
Propelling it down to the eel grass and the mud
Where once more on its own errantry it could go,
Compelled by will or hunger, wish or need,
Driven through regions my man's eyes never saw.

THE OCTOPUS

There are many monsters that a glassen surface
Restrains. And none more sinister
Than vision asleep in the eye's tight translucence.
Rarely it seeks now to unloose
Its diamonds. Having divined how drab a prison
The purest mortal tissue is,
Rarely it wakes. Unless, coaxed out by lusters
Extraordinary, like the octopus
From the gloom of its tank half-swimming
    half-drifting
Toward anything fair, a handkerchief
Or child's face dreaming near the glass, the writher
Advances in a godlike wreath
Of its own wrath. Chilled by such fragile reeling
A hundred blows of a boot-heel
Shall not quell, the dreamer wakes and hungers.
Percussive pulses, drum or gong,
Build in his skull their loud entrancement,
Volutions of a Hindu dance.
His hands move clumsily in the first conventional
Gestures of assent.
He is willing to undergo the volition and fervor
Of many fleshlike arms, observe

These in their holiness of indirection
Destroy, adore, evolve, reject –
Till on glass rigid with his own seizure
At length the sucking jewels freeze.

THE KRAKEN

Below the thunders of the upper deep;
Far far beneath in the abysmal sea,
His ancient, dreamless, uninvited sleep
The Kraken sleepeth: faintest sunlights flee
About his shadowy sides: above him swell
Huge sponges of millennial growth and height;
And far away into the sickly light,
From many a wondrous grot and secret cell
Unnumber'd and enormous polypi
Winnow with giant fins the slumbering green.
There he hath lain for ages and will lie
Battening upon huge seaworms in his sleep,
Until the latter fire shall heat the deep;
Then once by men and angels to be seen,
In roaring he shall rise and on the surface die.

THE WHALE
from Physiologus

Now I will fashion   the tale of a fish,
With wise wit singing   in measured strains
The song of the Great Whale.   Often unwittingly
Ocean-mariners   meet with this monster,
Fastitocalon,   fierce and menacing,
The Great Sea-Swimmer   of the ocean-streams.
Like a rough rock   is the Whale's appearance,
Or as if there were swaying   by the shore of the sea
A great mass of sedge   in the midst of the sand dunes;
So it seems to sailors   they see an island,
And they firmly fasten   their high-prowed ships
With anchor-ropes   to the land that is no land,
Hobble their sea-steeds   at ocean's end,
Land bold on the island   and leave their barks
Moored at the water's edge   in the wave's embrace.
There they encamp,   the sea-weary sailors,
Fearing no danger.   They kindle a fire;
High on the island   the hot flames blaze
And joy returns   to travel-worn hearts
Eager for rest.   Then, crafty in evil,
When the Whale feels the sailors   are fully set
And firmly lodged,   enjoying fair weather,
Suddenly with his prey   Ocean's Guest plunges
Down in the salt wave   seeking the depths,

In the hall of death   drowning sailors and ships.

Such is the manner of demons,   the devils' way,
Luring from virtue,   inciting to lust,
By secret power   deceiving men's souls
That they may seek help   at the hands of their foes
And, fixed in sin,   find abode with the Fiend.
Sly and deceitful,   when the Devil perceives
Out of hell-torment   that each of mankind,
Of the race of men,   is bound with his ring,
Then with cunning craft   the Dark Destroyer
Takes proud and humble   who here on earth
Through sin did his will.   Seizing them suddenly
Shrouded in darkness,   estranged from good,
He seeks out hell,   the bottomless abyss
In the misty gloom;   even as the Great Whale
Who drowns the mariners,   sea-steeds and men.

A second trait has he,   the proud Sea-Thrasher,
Even more marvellous: when hunger torments
And the fierce Water-Monster   is fain of food,
Then the Ocean-Warden   opens his mouth,
Unlocks his wide jaws,   and a winsome odour
Comes from his belly;   other kinds of fish
Are deceived thereby,   all eagerly swimming
To where the sweet fragrance   comes flowing forth.
In unwary schools   they enter within
Till the wide mouth is filled.   Then swiftly the Whale
Over his sea-prey   snaps his grim jaws.

So is it with him   in this transient time
Who takes heed to his life   too late and too little,
Letting vain delights   through their luring fragrance
Ensnare his soul   till he slips away,
Soiled with sin,   from the King of glory.
Before them the Devil   after death's journey
Throws open hell   for all who in folly
Fulfilled the lying   lusts of the flesh
Against the law.   But when the Wily One,
Expert in evil,   has brought into bonds
In the burning heat   those cleaving to him
Laden with sins,   who during their life-days
Did his bidding,   on them after death
His savage jaws   he snaps together,
The gates of hell.   Who gather there
Know no retreat,   no return out thence,
Any more than the fishes   swimming the sea
Can escape from the grip   of the Great Whale.
    Therefore by every means   (should every man
Serve the Lord God)   and strive against devils
By words and works,   that we may behold
The King of glory.   In this transient time
Let us seek for peace   and healing at His hands,
That we in grace may dwell   with Him so dear
And have His bliss   and blessedness for ever!

182   ANON. (ANGLO-SAXON)
     TRANSLATED BY CHARLES W. KENNEDY

LEVIATHAN

This is the black sea-brute bulling through
    wave-wrack,
Ancient as ocean's shifting hills, who in sea-toils
Travelling, who furrowing the salt acres
Heavily, his wake hoary behind him,
Shoulders spouting, the fist of his forehead
Over wastes gray-green crashing, among horses
    unbroken
From bellowing fields, past bone-wreck of vessels,
Tide-ruin, wash of lost bodies bobbing
No longer sought for, and islands of ice gleaming,
Who ravening the rank flood, wave-marshalling,
Overmastering the dark sea-marches, finds home
And harvest. Frightening to foolhardiest
Mariners, his size were difficult to describe:
The hulk of him is like hills heaving,
Dark, yet as crags of drift-ice, crowns cracking in
    thunder,
Like land's self by night black-looming, surf churning
    and trailing
Along his shores' rushing, shoal-water boding
About the dark of his jaws; and who should moor at his
    edge
And fare on afoot would find gates of no gardens,
But the hill of dark underfoot diving,

Closing overhead, the cold deep, and drowning.
He is called Leviathan, and named for rolling,
First created he was of all creatures,
He has held Jonah three days and nights,
He is that curling serpent that in ocean is,
Sea-fright he is, and the shadow under the earth.
Days there are, nonetheless, when he lies
Like an angel, although a lost angel
On the waste's unease, no eye of man moving,
Bird hovering, fish flashing, creature whatever
Who after him came to herit earth's emptiness.
Froth at flanks seething soothes to stillness,
Waits; with one eye he watches
Dark of night sinking last, with one eye dayrise
As at first over foaming pastures. He makes no cry
Though that light is a breath. The sea curling,
Star-climbed, wind-combed, cumbered with itself still
As at first it was, is the hand not yet contented
Of the Creator. And he waits for the world to begin.

A JELLY-FISH

Visible, invisible,
   a fluctuating charm
an amber-tinctured amethyst
   inhabits it, your arm
approaches and it opens
   and it closes; you had meant
to catch it and it quivers;
   you abandon your intent.

SEAL LULLABY

Oh! hush thee, my baby, the night is behind us,
    And black are the waters that sparkled so green.
The moon, o'er the combers, looks downward to find
      us
    At rest in the hollows that rustle between.
Where billow meets billow, there soft be thy pillow;
    Ah, weary wee flipperling, curl at thy ease!
The storm shall not wake thee, nor shark overtake
      thee,
    Asleep in the arms of the slow-swinging seas.

DOLPHINS
from Halieutica

Dolphins were Men, (Tradition hands the Tale)
Laborious Swains bred on the *Tuscan* Vale:
Transform'd by *Bacchus*, and by *Neptune* lov'd,
They all the Pleasures of the Deep improv'd.
When new-made Fish the God's Command obey'd,
Plung'd in the Waves, and untry'd Fins displayed,
No further Change relenting *Bacchus* wrought,
Nor have the *Dolphins* all the Man forgot;
The conscious Soul retains her former Thought.
When painful Throws, (for Twins the *Dolphins* bear)
And finish'd Time brings forth the Princely Pair,
They round their Parent frisk, sport by her Side;
Oft in her Mouth the little Wantons hide
She glad receives, with watchful Eye attends,
Directs their Motions, and from Harm defends;
Exulting leaps, and feels the Mother's Joy,
When with close Kiss she hugs the dandled Boy.
Then suckling gives to each the swelling Breast,
By partial Heav'n with Gifts uncommon blest.
The *Dolphin's* Paps a luscious Milk produce,
Hourly distending with secreted Juice.
But when her Young are grown to just Encrease,
And stronger Fins can wrestle with the Seas,
She to more useful Arts directs the Way,
And shows to vault the Waves, and chace the Prey.

What pleasing Wonders charm the Sailor's sight,
When Calms the *Dolphins* to their Sports invite!
As jovial Swains in tuneful Measure tread,
And leave their rounding Pressures on the Mead;
So they in circling Dance, with wanton Ease
Pursue each other round the furrow'd Seas,
With rapid Force the curling Streams divide,
Add to the Waves, and drive the slow-pac'd Tide.
The Parent *Dolphins*, with suspicious Care,
Of casual Harms, and guilty Floods beware,
Move cautious on behind, and guard the Rear.

TRANSLATED BY WILLIAM DIAPER

THE WOES OF THE CRAB
"BEGGAR SONG"

In the Bay of Naniwa –
Naniwa of the flashing waves –
I huddle in the home I made.
A reed-crab, my lord commands me,
So they say, but know not the cause.
Yet I know well the circumstance.
As singer am I summoned?
As flutist am I summoned?
As harpist am I summoned?
But, obeying his commands,
When today becomes tomorrow
I come to Morrow Town:
Though downed, I reach Downham:
And while I have no stick,
I find myself on Stafford Plain.
Going in the Eastern Gate
Of the castle's inner wall,
I hear my lord's commands.
Like haltered horse, I am tethered:
Like an ox, twine binds my nose.
Then from the hillside he brings
Five hundred strips of elm-tree bark,
Hangs it to dry in the shining sun,
Treads it in a Chinese mortar,

Pounds it with the garden pestle.
Thick, first-dripped salt from Naniwa Bay –
Naniwa of the flashing waves –
And swift-made potter's jars he brings.
Then he smears my eyes with salt
And says, 'A tasty dish indeed.'

WINGS OVER
THE WATER

EGRETS

In cloaks of snow, hairs snow-white, and beaks of blue
     jade,
They gather to hunt for fish, their reflection in the
     brook;
Startled they fly off, cast their distant shadows on
     green hills.
And all the blossoms of a pear tree fall in the evening
     breeze.

TU MU   193
TRANSLATED BY IRVING Y. LO

TO A WATERFOWL

Whither, 'midst falling dew,
While glow the heavens with the last steps of day
Far, through their rosy depths, dost thou pursue
Thy solitary way?

Vainly the fowler's eye
Might mark thy distant flight to do thee wrong,
As, darkly painted on the crimson sky,
Thy figure floats along.

Seek'st thou the plashy brink
Of weedy lake, or marge of river wide,
Or where the rocking billows rise and sink
On the chafed ocean side?

There is a Power whose care
Teaches thy way along that pathless coast, —
The desert and illimitable air, —
Lone wandering, but not lost.

All day thy wings have fanned,
At that far height, the cold thin atmosphere,
Yet stoop not, weary, to the welcome land,
    Though the dark night is near.

And soon that toil shall end,
Soon shalt thou find a summer home, and rest,
And scream among thy fellows; reeds shall bend,
    Soon, o'er thy sheltered nest.

Thou'rt gone, the abyss of heaven
Hath swallow'd up thy form; yet, on my heart
Deeply hath sunk the lesson thou hast given,
    And shall not soon depart.

He, who, from zone to zone,
Guides through the boundless sky thy certain flight
In the long way that I must tread alone,
    Will lead my steps aright.

WILLIAM CULLEN BRYANT

MIGRATING BIRDS

Where the Rhine loses his majestic force
In Belgian plains, won from the raging deep
By diligence amazing and the strong
Unconquerable hand of liberty,
The stork-assembly meets, for many a day
Consulting deep and various ere they take
Their arduous voyage through the liquid sky.
And now, their route designed, their leaders chose,
Their tribes adjusted, cleaned their vigorous wings,
And many a circle, many a short essay,
Wheeled round and round, in congregation full
The figured flight ascends, and, riding high
The aerial billows, mixes with the clouds.
    Or, where the Northern Ocean in vast whirls
Boils round the naked melancholy isles
Of farthest Thule, and the Atlantic surge
Pours in among the stormy Hebrides,
Who can recount what transmigrations there
Are annual made? what nations come and go?
And how the living clouds on clouds arise,
Infinite wings! till all the plume–dark air
And rude resounding shore are one wild cry?

FLAMINGO

Flamingo, what has brought you here?
Has no-one told you that the cranes
In this land have usurped your name?
Why have you come? Go home again
Before some fool calls you a crane.

ANON. (SANSKRIT)

TRANSLATED BY JOHN BROUGH

THE FLAMINGOS
Jardin des Plantes, Paris

With all the subtle paints of Fragonard
no more of their red and white could be expressed
than someone would convey about his mistress
by telling you, "She was lovely, lying there

still soft with sleep." They rise above the green
grass and lightly sway on their long pink stems,
side by side, like enormous feathery blossoms,
seducing (more seductively than Phryne)

themselves; till, necks curling, they sink their large
pale eyes into the softness of their down,
where apple-red and jet-black lie concealed.

A shriek of envy shakes the parrot cage;
but *they* stretch out, astonished, and one by one
stride into their imaginary world.

TRANSLATED BY STEPHEN MITCHELL

WATER FOWL

'Let me be allowed the aid of verse to describe the evolutions which these visitants sometimes perform, on a fine day towards the close of winter.' – EXTRACT FROM THE AUTHOR'S BOOK ON THE LAKES.

Mark how the feathered tenants of the flood,
With grace of motion that might scarcely seem
Inferior to angelical, prolong
Their curious pastime! shaping in mid air
(And sometimes with ambitious wing that soars
High as the level of the mountain-tops)
A circuit ampler than the lake beneath –
Their own domain; but ever, while intent
On tracing and retracing that large round,
Their jubilant activity evolves
Hundreds of curves and circlets, to and fro,
Upward and downward, progress intricate
Yet unperplexed, as if one spirit swayed
Their indefatigable flight. 'Tis done –
Ten times, or more I fancied it had ceased;
But lo! the vanished company again
Ascending; they approach – I hear their wings,
Faint, faint at first; and then an eager sound,
Past in a moment – and as faint again!

They tempt the sun to sport amid their plumes;
They tempt the water, or the gleaming ice,
To show them a fair image; 'tis themselves,
Their own fair forms, upon the glimmering plain
Painted more soft and fair as they descend
Almost to touch; – then up again aloft,
Up with a sally and a flash of speed,
As if they scorned both resting-place and rest!

THE SWAN

This laboring through what is still undone,
as though, legs bound, we hobbled along the way,
is like the awkward walking of the swan.

And dying – to let go, no longer feel
the solid ground we stand on every day –
is like his anxious letting himself fall

into the water, which receives him gently
and which, as though with reverence and joy,
draws back past him in streams on either side;
while, infinitely silent and aware,
in his full majesty and ever more
indifferent, he condescends to glide.

RAINER MARIA RILKE
TRANSLATED BY STEPHEN MITCHELL

THE DYING SWAN

The plain was grassy, wild and bare,
Wide, wild, and open to the air,
Which had built up everywhere
An under-roof of doleful grey.
With an inner voice the river ran,
Adown it floated a dying swan,
And loudly did lament.
It was the middle of the day.
Even the weary wind went on,
And took the reed-tops as it went.

Some blue peaks in the distance rose,
And white against the cold-white sky,
Shone out their crowning snows.
One willow over the river wept,
And shook the wave as the wind did sigh;
Above in the wind was the swallow,
Chasing itself at its own wild will,
And far thro' the marish green and still
The tangled water-courses slept,
Shot over with purple, and green, and yellow.

The wild swan's death-hymn took the soul
Of that waste place with joy
Hidden in sorrow: at first to the ear
The warble was low, and full and clear;
And floating about the under-sky,
Prevailing in weakness, the coronach stole
Sometimes afar, and sometimes anear;
But anon her awful jubilant voice,
With a music strange and manifold,
Flow'd forth on a carol free and bold;

As when a mighty people rejoice
With shawms and cymbals, and harps of gold,
And the tumult of their acclaim is roll'd
Thro' the open gates of the city afar,
To the shepherd who watcheth the evening star.
And the creeping mosses and clambering weeds,
And the willow-branches hoar and dank,
And the wavy swell of the soughing reeds,
And the wave-worn horns of the echoing bank,
And the silvery marish-flowers that throng
The desolate creeks and pools among,
Were flooded over with eddying song.

ALFRED, LORD TENNYSON

CREATURES
SMALL

FIREFLIES

Fireflies throw
love winks
to their kind
on the dark, glow
without heat,
their day bodies
common beetles.
In a planetarium
of the mind
sparks lit
when logic has gone
down
faint in the dawn
of intellect.
Instinct
makes luminous
the insect.
Idea's anonymous
ordinary mark,
that cryptic
in daylight crept,
can rise an asterisk
astonishing others out.

If the secret
of the dark
be kept,
an eagerness
in smallest, fiercest
hints
can scintillate.

THE MOWER TO THE GLOWWORMS

1

Ye living lamps, by whose dear light
The nightingale does sit so late,
And studying all the summer-night,
Her matchless songs does meditate;

2

Ye country comets, that portend
No war, nor prince's funeral,
Shining unto no higher end
Than to presage the grass's fall;

3

Ye glowworms, whose officious flame
To wand'ring mowers shows the way,
That in the night have lost their aim,
And after foolish fires do stray;

4

Your courteous lights in vain you waste,
Since *Juliana* here is come,
For she my mind hath so displaced
That I shall never find my home.

ANDREW MARVELL

THE GRASSHOPPER:
To My Noble Friend, Mr. Charles Cotton

O thou that swing'st upon the waving hair
   Of some well-fillèd oaten-beard,
Drunk every night with a delicious tear
   Dropped thee from heaven, where now thou art
     reared.

The joys of earth and air are thine entire,
   That with thy feet and wings dost hop and fly;
And when thy poppy works thou dost retire
   To thy carved acorn-bed to lie.

Up with the day, the sun thou welcom'st then,
   Sport'st in the gilt-plaits of his beams,
And all these merry days mak'st merry men,
   Thyself, and melancholy streams.

But ah, the sickle! golden ears are cropped;
   Ceres and Bacchus bid good-night;
Sharp frosty fingers all your flowers have topped
   And what scythes spared, winds shave off quite.

Poor verdant fool! and now green ice! thy joys,
   Large and as lasting as thy perch of grass,

Bid us lay in 'gainst winter rain, and poise
 Their floods with an o'er flowing glass.

Thou best of men and friends! we will create
 A genuine summer in each other's breast;
And spite of this cold time and frozen fate
 Thaw us a warm seat to our rest.

Our sacred hearths shall burn eternally
 As vestal flames; the north-wind, he
Shall strike his frost-stretched wings, dissolve and fly
 This Etna in epitome.

Dropping December shall come weeping in,
 Bewail the usurping of his reign;
But when in showers of old Greek we begin
 Shall cry he hath his crown again!

Night as clear Hesper shall our tapers whip
 From the light casements where we play,
And the dark hag from her black mantle strip,
 And stick there everlasting day.

Thus richer than untempted kings are we,
 That asking nothing, nothing need:
Thou Lord of all what seas embrace, yet he
 That wants himself is poor indeed.

RICHARD LOVELACE

                    r-p-o-p-h-e-s-s-a-g-r
          who
a)s w(e loo)k
upnowgath
          PPEGORHRASS
                              eringint(o-
aThe):l
      eA
        !p:
S   a
                  (r
rIvInG   .gRrEaPsPhOs)
                                    to
rea(be)rran(com)gi(e)ngly
,grasshopper;

GRASSHOPPER

  G

   G

    G

     GOLD Goldsmith's ...

     Runner? No,

      All

       Summer a topflight

       Scholar of stalks, in

        Herringbone (*spiffy!*) plus-fours,

         Odd-lot jumper, clawed plimsolls,

           aviators –

         Parsing the leaflet's old tag:

         PERTINAX AUREUM

         ERRORQUE

        RERUM

        R

         R

          R

           R

          R

           R

THE GRASSHOPPER AND CRICKET

The poetry of earth is never dead;
 When all the birds are faint with the hot sun,
 And hide in cooling trees, a voice will run
From hedge to hedge about the new-mown mead;
That is the Grasshopper's – he takes the lead
 In summer luxury, – he has never done
 With his delights; for when tired out with fun
He rests at ease beneath some pleasant weed.
The poetry of earth is ceasing never:
 On a lone winter evening, when the frost
  Has wrought a silence, from the stove there
   shrills
The Cricket's song, in warmth increasing ever,
 And seems to one in drowsiness half lost,
  The Grasshopper's among some grassy hills.

CICADAS

The cicadas sing
in the twilight
of my mountain village . . .
tonight, no one
will visit save the wind

ONO NO KOMACHI
TRANSLATED BY JANE HIRSHFIELD
AND MARIKO ARATANI

CRICKET HEARD

Although
the cricket's song
has no words,
still,
it sounds like sorrow

CICADAS

Dew-rinsed:
their pure notes
carry far.

Windblown:
as dry, fasting leaves
are blown.

Chirr after chirr,
as if in unison.

But each perches
on its one branch,
alone.

XUE TAO
TRANSLATED BY JEANNE LARSEN

A FLYING FLOWER

Fallen flower I see
Returning to its branch –
Ah! a butterfly.

ARAKIDA MORITAKE
TRANSLATED BY GEOFFREY BOWNAS
AND ANTHONY THWAITE

BUTTERFLY

Butterfly, the wind blows sea-ward, strong beyond the
    garden wall!
Butterfly, why do you settle on my shoe, and sip the
    dirt on my shoe,
Lifting your veined wings, lifting them? big white
    butterfly!

Already it is October, and the wind blows strong to the
    sea
from the hills where snow must have fallen, the wind is
    polished with snow.
Here in the garden, with red geraniums, it is warm, it is
    warm
but the wind blows strong to sea-ward, white butterfly,
    content on my shoe!

Will you go, will you go from my warm house?
Will you climb on your big soft wings, black-dotted,
as up an invisible rainbow, an arch
till the wind slides you sheer from the arch-crest
and in a strange level fluttering you go out to sea-
    ward, white speck!

Farewell, farewell, lost soul!
you have melted in the crystalline distance,
it is enough! I saw you vanish into air.

D. H. LAWRENCE   219

TO A BUTTERFLY

Already in midsummer
I miss your feet and fur.
Poor simple creature that you were,
What have you become!

Your slender person curled
About an apple twig
Rebounding to the winds' clear jig
Gave up the world

In favor of obscene
Gray matter, rode that ark
Until (as at the chance remark
Of Father Sheen)

Shining awake to slough
Your old life. And soon four
Dapper stained glass windows bore
You up – *Enough.*

Goodness, how tired one grows
Just looking through a prism:
Allegory, symbolism.
I've tried, Lord knows,

To keep from seeing double,
Blushed for whenever I did,
Prayed like a boy my cheek be hid
By manly stubble.

I caught you in a net
And first pierced your disguise
How many years ago? Time flies,
I am not yet

Proof against rigmarole.
Those frail wings, those antennae!
The day you hover without any
Tincture of soul,

Red monarch, swallowtail,
Will be the day my own
Wiles gather dust. Each will have flown
The other's jail.

A NOISELESS, PATIENT SPIDER

A noiseless patient spider,
I mark'd where on a little promontory it stood isolated,
Mark'd how to explore the vacant vast surrounding,
It launched forth filament, filament, filament, out of
    itself,
Ever unreeling them, ever tirelessly speeding them.

And you O my soul where you stand,
Surrounded, detached, in measureless oceans of space,
Ceaselessly musing, venturing, throwing, seeking the
    spheres to connect them,
Till the bridge you will need be form'd, till the ductile
    anchor hold,
Till the gossamer thread you fling catch somewhere, O
    my soul.

THE STUDY OF A SPIDER

From holy flower to holy flower
Thou weavest thine unhallowed bower.
The harmless dewdrops, beaded thin,
Ripple along thy ropes of sin.
Thy house a grave, a gulf thy throne
Affright the fairies every one.
Thy winding sheets are grey and fell,
Imprisoning with nets of hell
The lovely births that winnow by,
Winged sisters of the rainbow sky:
Elf-darlings, fluffy, bee-bright things,
And owl-white moths with mealy wings,
And tiny flies, as gauzy thin
As e'er were shut electrum in.
These are thy death spoils, insect ghoul,
With their dear life thy fangs are foul.
Thou felon anchorite of pain
Who sittest in a world of slain.
Hermit, who tunest song unsweet
To heaving wing and writhing feet.
A glutton of creation's sighs,
Miser of many miseries.
Toper, whose lonely feasting chair
Sways in inhospitable air.
The board is bare, the bloated host

Drinks to himself toast after toast.
His lips requires no goblet brink,
But like a weasel must he drink.
The vintage is as old as time
And bright as sunset, pressed and prime.

Ah venom mouth and shaggy thighs
And paunch grown sleek with sacrifice,
Thy dolphin back and shoulders round
Coarse-hairy as some goblin hound
Whom a hag rides to sabbath on,
While shuddering stars in fear grow wan.
Thou palace priest of treachery,
Thou type of selfish lechery,
I break the toils around thy head
And from their gibbets take thy dead.

CLOCK-A-CLAY (The Lady Bug)

In the cowslip peeps I lie
Hidden from the buzzing fly,
While green grass beneath me lies
Pearled wi' dew like fishes' eyes.
Here I lie, a clock-a-clay,
Waiting for the time o' day.

While grassy forests quake surprise,
And the wild wind sobs and sighs,
My gold home rocks as like to fall
On its pillar green and tall;
When the parting rain drives by
Clock-a-clay keeps warm and dry.

Day by day and night by night
All the week I hide from sight.
In the cowslip peeps I lie,
In rain and dew still warm and dry.
Day and night, and night and day,
Red, black-spotted clock-a-clay.

My home it shakes in wind and shows
Pale green pillar topped wi' flowers,
Bending at the wild wind's breath
Till I touch the grass beneath.
Here I live, lone clock-a-clay,
Watching for the time of day.

JOHN CLARE

DRAGONFLY

Itinerant clarinet
A celesta comb tunes with wings:
Bayadere on the Moor's back,
Amusing a fuzzy crowd busy
In Admiralty Square.

Its flight? Oh, the baggy clown's,
Mooning by day, collapsing at night
In a tiny starpatched sky loft
Where successive dreams muster
Scimitars, a fanfare of palms . . .

Shrovetide masqueraders
In a mob of selves that others see –
Devil-and-Goat, Eye-on-Broomstick,
Goblin tableaux over dome and cross.
They cannot scare but kill the clown.

One more quiver in that arrow.
Out of its wits, it wobbles, still.
– It's then the ghost appears, high
Over the plot, and on its particulars.
On the membraned leaf.

On the loosestrife's whips.
On the air. On my lips.

ARACHNE

I watch her in the corner there,
As, restless, bold, and unafraid,
She slips and floats along the air
Till all her subtile house is made.

Her home, her bed, her daily food
All from that hidden store she draws;
She fashions it and knows it good,
By instinct's strong and sacred laws.

No tenuous threads to weave her nest,
She seeks and gathers there or here;
But spins it from her faithful breast,
Renewing still, till leaves are sere.

Then, worn with toil, and tired of life,
In vain her shining traps are set.
Her frost hath hushed the insect strife
And gilded flies her charm forget.

But swinging in the snares she spun,
She sways to every wintry wind:
Her joy, her toil, her errand done,
Her corse the sport of storms unkind.

Poor sister of the spinster clan!
I too from out my store within
My daily life and living plan,
My home, my rest, my pleasure spin.

I know thy heart when heartless hands
Sweep all that hard-earned web away:
Destroy its pearled and glittering bands,
And leave thee homeless by the way.

I know thy peace when all is done.
Each anchored thread, each tiny knot,
Soft shining in the autumn sun;
A sheltered, silent, tranquil lot.

I know what thou hast never known,
– Sad presage to a soul allowed; –
That not for life I spin, alone.
But day by day I spin my shroud.

ALL CREATURES

THE SONG OF THE BEASTS
(*Sung, on one night, in the cities, in the darkness*)

Come away! Come away!
Ye are sober and dull through the common day,
But now it is night!
It is shameful night, and God is asleep!
(Have you not felt the quick fires that creep
Through the hungry flesh, and the lust of delight,
And hot secrets of dreams that day cannot say?) ....
... The house is dumb;
The night calls out to you.... Come, ah, come!
Down the dim stairs, through the creaking door,
Naked, crawling on hands and feet
– It is meet! it is meet!
Ye are men no longer, but less and more,
Beast and God.... Down the lampless street,
By little black ways, and secret places,
In darkness and mire,
Faint laughter around, and evil faces
By the star-glint seen – ah! follow with us!
For the darkness whispers a blind desire,
And the fingers of night are amorous....
Keep close as we speed,
Though mad whispers woo you, and hot hands cling,
And the touch and the smell of bare flesh sting,
Soft flank by your flank, and side brushing side –

Tonight never heed!
Unswerving and silent follow with me,
Till the city ends sheer,
And the crook'd lanes open wide,
Out of the voices of night,
Beyond lust and fear,
To the level waters of moonlight,
To the level waters, quiet and clear,
To the black unresting plains of the calling sea.

TENANTS OF PARADISE
from Paradise Lost, IV

About them frisking played
All beasts of the earth, since wild, and of all chase
In wood or wilderness, forest or den;
Sporting the lion ramped, and in his paw
Dandled the kid; bears, tigers, ounces, pards,
Gamboled before them, the unwieldy elephant
To make them mirth used all his might, and wreathed
His lithe proboscis; close thew serpent sly
Insinuating, wove with Gordian twine
His braided train, and of his fatal guile
Gave proof unheeded; others on the grass
Couched, and now filled with pasture gazing sat,
Or bedward ruminating . . .

TENANTS OF AN ABANDONED CASTLE
from "Grongar Hill"

'Tis now the raven's bleak abode;
'Tis now the apartment of the toad;
And there the fox securely feeds;
And there the poisonous adder breeds
Conceal'd in ruins, moss and weeds ...

ECOLOGY OF THE VILLAGE
from The Deserted Village

Sweet was the sound when oft at evening's close,
Up yonder hill the village murmur rose;
There as I past with careless steps and slow,
The mingling notes came softened from below;
The swain responsive as the milk-maid sung,
The sober herd that lowed to meet their young,
The noisy geese that gabbled o'er the pool,
The playful children just loose from school,
The watch-dog's voice that bayed the whispering
      wind,
And the loud laugh that spoke the vacant mind,
These all in sweet confusion sought the shade,
And filled each pause the nightingale had made.

OLIVER GOLDSMITH

ANIMALS ENJOYING LIFE
from The Task, VI

The heart is hard in nature, and unfit
For human fellowship, as being void
Of sympathy, and therefore dead alike
To love and friendship both, that is not pleased
With sight of animals enjoying life,
Nor feels their happiness augment his own.
The bounding fawn, that darts across the glade
When none pursues, through mere delight of heart,
And spirits buoyant with excess of glee;
The horse as wanton, and almost as fleet,
That skims the spacious meadow at full speed,
Then stops and snorts, and, throwing high his heels,
Starts to the voluntary race again;
The very kine that gambol at high noon,
The total herd receiving first from one
That leads the dance a summons to be gay,
Though wild their strange vagaries, and uncouth
Their efforts, yet resolved with one consent
To give such act and utterance as they may
To ecstasy too big to be suppressed;

These, and a thousand images of bliss,
With which kind nature graces every scene,
Where cruel man defeats not her design,
Impart to the benevolent, who wish
All that are capable of pleasure pleased.
A far superior happiness to theirs,
The comfort of a reasonable joy.

SIGNS OF STORM

With broadened nostrils to the sky upturned,
The conscious heifer snuffs the stormy gale.
Even, as the matron, at her nightly task,
With pensive labour draws the flaxen thread,
The wasted taper and the crackling flame
Foretell the blast. But chief the plumy race,
The tenants of the sky, its changes speak.
Retiring from the downs, where all day long
They picked their scanty fare, a blackening train
Of clamorous rooks thick-urge their weary flight,
And seek the closing shelter of the grove.
Assiduous, in his bower, the wailing owl
Plies his sad song. The cormorant on high
Wheels from the deep, and screams along the land.
Loud shrieks the soaring hern; and with wild wing
The circling sea-fowl cleave the flaky clouds.
Ocean, unequal pressed, with broken tide
And blind commotion heaves; while from the shore,
Eat into caverns by the restless wave,
And forest-rustling mountain comes a voice
That, solemn-sounding, bids the world prepare.

SIGNS OF RAIN
from Georgics, Book I

Wet weather seldom hurts the most unwise;
So plain the signs, such prophets are the skies.
The wary crane foresees it first, and sails
Above the storm, and leaves the lowly vales;
The cow looks up, and from afar can find
The change of heav'n, and snuffs it in the wind;
The swallow skims the river's wat'ry face;
The frogs renew the croaks of their loquacious race;
The careful ant her secret cell forsakes,
And drags her eggs along the narrow tracks:
At either horn the rainbow drinks the flood;
Huge flocks of rising rooks forsake their food,
And, crying, seek the shelter of the wood.
Besides, the sev'ral sorts of wat'ry fowls
That swim the seas, or haunt the standing pools,
The swans that sail along the silver flood,
And dive with stretching necks to search their food,
Then lave their backs with sprinkling dews in vain,
And stem the stream to meet the promis'd rain.
The crow with clam'rous cries the show'r demands,
And single stalks along the desert sands.

HOW THEY COMMUNICATE

Even the dumb beasts,
The inarticulate animals, make sounds
That indicate emotions, fear, or pain,
Or even happiness. This is obvious.
Bloodhounds, when you annoy them, start by growling
Inside their jowls, or bare their teeth and snarl,
Crescendo to the loud full-throated bark.
Again, the sounds are different when they nuzzle
Their puppies, paw them around in play, pretend
To nip, or gobble them up, from when they howl
In some deserted house, or slink away
In terror of a whipping. Is there not
A difference in the whinny of a stallion
Loose with the mares, from when he snorts a challenge
To other studs, or makes a nickering sound
Just for the hell of it? Birds also wheel,
The hawks, the gulls, the ospreys, calling loud,
Skimming the waves in search of food, but giving
A different cry when they must fight to keep
Their prey from other birds. And weather, too,
Can make a difference – ravens and crows
Are not the same when prophesying rain
As when they summon wind. If animals,

Dumb beasts, can utter such dissimilar sounds
For different feelings, mortal man must be
At least as able by his voice to mark
Distinctions between objects.

LUCRETIUS

TRANSLATED BY ROLFE HUMPHRIES

WHAT THEY MEAN

A Robin Red breast in a Cage
Puts all Heaven in a Rage
A dove house filled with doves & Pigeons
Shudders Hell thro all its regions
A dog starvd at his Masters Gate
Predicts the ruin of the State
A Horse misusd upon the Road
Calls to Heaven for Human blood
Each outcry of the hunted Hare
A fibre from the Brain does tear
A Skylark wounded in the wing
A Cherubim does cease to sing
The Game Cock clipd & armd for fight
Does the Rising Sun affright
Every Wolfs & Lions howl
Raises from Hell a Human Soul
The wild deer wandring here & there
Keeps the Human Soul from Care
The Lamb misusd breeds Public strife
And yet forgives the Butchers Knife
The Bat that flits at close of Eve
Has left the Brain that wont Believe
The Owl that calls upon the Night
Speaks the Unbelievers fright

He who shall hurt the little Wren
Shall never be beloved by Men
He who the Ox to wrath has movd
Shall never be by Woman lovd
The wanton Boy that kills the Fly
Shall feel the Spiders enmity
He who torments the Chafers sprite
Weaves a Bower in endless Night
The Catterpiller on the Leaf
Repeats to thee thy Mothers grief
Kill not the Moth nor Butterfly
For the Last Judgment draweth nigh
He who shall train the Horse to War
Shall never pass the Polar Bar
The Beggers Dog & Widows Cat
Feed them & thou wilt grow fat
The Gnat that sings his Summers song
Poison gets from Slanders tongue
The poison of the Snake & Newt
Is the sweat of Envys Foot
The Poison of the Honey Bee
Is the Artists Jealousy . . .

WILLIAM BLAKE

THE CREATURES REST

Now sleep mountain-top and chasm
headland and ravine,
creeping kinds that emerge from the black earth
beasts who roam the hillside, the race of bees,
and creatures submerged in the purple sea
now sleep, and tribes,
too, of the wide-winged birds.

ADAM'S TASK

And Adam gave names to all cattle, and
to the fowl of the air, and to every beast
of the field . . . GEN. 2:20

Thou, paw-paw-paw; thou, glurd; thou, spotted
   Glurd; thou, whitestap, lurching through
The high-grown brush; thou, pliant-footed,
   Implex; thou, awagabu.

Every burrower, each flier
   Came for the name he had to give:
Gay, first work, ever to be prior,
   Not yet sunk to primitive.

Thou, verdle; thou, McFleery's pomma;
   Thou; thou; thou – three types of grawl;
Thou, flisket; thou, kabasch; thou, comma-
   Eared mashawk; thou, all; thou, all.

Were, in a fire of becoming,
   Laboring to be burned away,
Then work, half-measuring, half-humming,
   Would be as serious as play.

Thou, pambler; thou, rivarn; thou, greater
　　Wherret, and thou, lesser one;
Thou, sproal; thou, zant; thou, lily-eater.
　　Naming's over. Day is done.

BEASTS

Beasts in their major freedom
Slumber in peace tonight. The gull on his ledge
Dreams in the guts of himself the moon-plucked waves
below,
And the sunfish leans on a stone, slept
By the lyric water,

In which the spotless feet
Of deer make dulcet splashes, and to which
The ripped mouse, safe in the owl's talon, cries
Concordance. Here there is no such harm
And no such darkness

As the selfsame moon observes
Where, warped in window-glass, it sponsors now
The werewolf's painful change. Turning his head away
On the sweaty bolster, he tries to remember
The mood of manhood,

But lies at last, as always,
Letting it happen, the fierce fur soft to his face,
Hearing with sharper ears the wind's exciting minors,
The leaves' panic, and the degradation
Of the heavy streams.

Meantime, at high windows
Far from thicket and pad-fall, suitors of excellence
Sigh and turn from their work to construe again the
painful
Beauty of heaven, the lucid moon
And the risen hunter,

Making such dreams for men
As told will break their hearts as always, bringing
Monsters into the city, crows on the public statues,
Navies fed to the fish in the dark
Unbridled waters.

INDEX OF AUTHORS